Brain Training for

This book is dedicated to Ide and Tass.

Brain Training for Babies

Fergus Lowe and Brigid Lowe

Hodder Education

338 Euston Road, London NW1 3BH.

Hodder Education is an Hachette UK company

First published in UK 2011 by Hodder Education

First published in US 2011 by The McGraw-Hill Companies, Inc.

This edition published 2011.

British Library Cataloguing in Publication Data: a catalogue record
for this title is available from the British Library.

Library of Congress Catalog Card Number: on file.

10 9 8 7 6 5 4 3 2 1

The publisher has used its best endeavours to ensure that any
website addresses referred to in this book are correct and active at
the time of going to press. However, the publisher and the author
have no responsibility for the websites and can make no guarantee
that a site will remain live or that the content will remain relevant,
decent or appropriate.

The publisher has made every effort to mark as such all words
which it believes to be trademarks. The publisher should also
like to make it clear that the presence of a word in the book,
whether marked or unmarked, in no way affects its legal status as
a trademark.

Every reasonable effort has been made by the publisher to trace the
copyright holders of material in this book. Any errors or omissions
should be notified in writing to the publisher, who will endeavour
to rectify the situation for any reprints and future editions.

Hachette UK's policy is to use papers that are natural, renewable
and recyclable products and made from wood grown in sustainable
forests. The logging and manufacturing processes are expected to
conform to the environmental regulations of the country of origin.

www.hoddereducation.co.uk

Typeset by MPS Limited, a Macmillan Company.

Printed in Great Britain by CPI Cox & Wyman, Reading.

Acknowledgments

Thanks to Pat and Catrin Lowe for untangling our thoughts and grammar once again. Thanks to Tass, for providing practical demonstrations of facts about baby intelligence, such as that a one-year-old can break into a dangerous locked cupboard in half the time it takes his mother find 'insert bullet points' in the menu. Thanks to Sean for being such a stalwart supporter of baby brain-training in both theory and practice. And thanks to Ide for being the sort of person who would inspire anyone to wonder about baby brains.

Disclaimer
The publisher accepts no liability for any consequences that arise from acting upon the advice or information contained within this book. If you have any concerns over your child's health you should seek the advice of a medical professional.

Contents

Meet the authors

Fergus Lowe is a Professor of Psychology and has been working on child development and behaviour for 40 years, much of the time as head of a leading UK Psychology Department, at Bangor in Wales. He has advised governments and other agencies on behaviour change and public policy, and his learning programmes for children are put in practice across the world. He has two grown-up daughters whose brains he helped train. He's happy with his efforts – they both seem to have turned out OK.

His elder daughter and co-author, Brigid Lowe, is a writer and full-time mother, and does not consider this a contradiction. She typed this book while nursing, and read the proofs while combing play-doh out of tangled curls. Before her daughter Ide (five years old) and son Tass (one year old) became a complete handful, she was a fellow of Trinity College, Cambridge. She has taught many brilliant students, but not one has tested, challenged and stimulated her own mind as much as Ide and Tass.

In addition to drawing upon all we know about the research on child psychology, the facts and ideas in the book were tested by turns on Tass or Ide, as we went along. Training their brains has been a joy and privilege, and it seems to us that the results are quite extraordinary. We are confident that, with a little work, you too will end up confident that you have the brainiest and generally most amazing babies in the world.

In one minute

Call centre put you on hold? Find a sweet spot on baby, and kiss it. Waiting for water to get hot? Blow a raspberry on their chin – twice.

Did you know that loving touch helps baby's body *and brain* to grow? The cascade of happy hormones triggered by nuzzles promotes brain growth and learning. The emotional bond between you, strengthened each time you bury your nose in your baby's chubby legs or stroke their velvety head, is essential for the growth of intelligence. Babies learn most from people they love, and who love them – from people who make them happy. *Brain Training for Babies* is all about loving and having fun.

You can make a big difference to your child's intelligence – but not just by choosing well-designed flash cards. The biggest difference depends on how you share the uncountable moments of ongoing life doing things like waiting for the microwave to beep, or the bus to show up. The way you change your baby's nappies will make more difference to their brain than any number of products 'designed by psychologists' to transform them into a prodigy.

Making the most of minutes isn't rocket science. You are biologically programmed to be a great baby trainer. But, in the rush of things, it's easy to lose precious moments.

This book will help you understand and wonder at babies' amazing achievements. Our tips will help you build on your fundamental love for your own baby to become a better brain trainer, and a better parent, every minute of every day.

Introduction: how you can help train your baby's brain

Who is this book for?

This book is for you if you want to raise an intelligent child – but it is also for you if you want a blissfully happy baby.

People sometimes talk as though these two goals were in tension with each other. The idea is that 'pushy parents' care more about their children's achievements than about their happiness.

Whether or not this makes sense when you are talking about older children, it certainly does not make sense when you are talking about babies. Setting out to train your baby's brain isn't a matter of putting them on a gruelling regime. It's about satisfying their deepest needs and desires. The most common reason a healthy baby cries is because they are not being given what they need to learn. Let your baby learn, as intensely as they want, and they will be happy. This sounds simple – but it requires energy and skill.

What will it take to train my baby's brain?

We humans are able to do the amazing things we do because human babies are such incredibly high-powered learners. Human babies have the capacity and the will to learn at a speed that is completely beyond any other animal – or, in fact, adult humans either! But human babies, more than the babies of any other species, need a lot of support to learn. That special sort of support must come from devoted people around them.

At first, baby cannot even sit up to see the world they need to learn about. They learn about the world through you. Both their emotional and intellectual development is dependent on your input – and the more time and effort you put in, the more your baby gains. This book is designed to help you make that effort, and help you channel your energy in ways that will be most stimulating for your baby.

How will this book help?

You may be amazed how exciting, but also demanding, it can be to keep up with your baby's needs for mental stimulation. It can feel as though their brain is an engine powered by a raging furnace that you must feed with coal as fast as you can.

So this book is designed not just to keep baby engaged, but also to support and motivate you. The targeted activities it suggests will help to keep you going, and to refresh your imagination and energy as your baby learns. They will help you keep up with your baby's amazing mental leaps.

That's the way you should see this book: as a way to keep both you and your baby happy and interested. We do not have a complete and proven recipe for programming your child to be a genius. Babies are too complex, and too bright, for anyone to construct such a thing. Anyone who thinks they have such a programme does not understand anything about the smartness of babies! Scientists are still learning about the amazing ways their minds grow. Often, as we will see, your own instincts will lead you towards the sort of behaviour they most need to help them learn. But this book's suggestions do draw on all the latest scientific evidence about what babies know, how they learn, and strategies that have been shown to work, or not to work, in helping them to make progress.

To train your baby, you need to understand it

This book is focused around specific games and activities that will help your baby learn, and help you learn about your baby. But each chapter also gives general information about the way baby's mind works and grows. This should help you shape your own daily behaviour in ways that benefit baby's mental development.

It's easy to see how this would be the case if you watch how adults help children with their physical development. As your baby grows, you will notice that people who don't see them on a daily basis often tend to get things wrong. Your baby is learning to reach out and grab, but Uncle Bob puts the rattle into their hand and curls their fingers round the handle. That's no fun! Your baby most enjoys playing with people who understand what we call their *zone of proximal development* – where they are at – that is, the range of stuff they are currently working on and might just be able to manage on their own, with a bit of help.

Understanding the way your baby's mind works and grows will help you appreciate just what your baby is achieving mentally during their first couple of years. Watching your baby's learning processes will fill you with fascination and wonder. You will tune in to the enormous mental strides behind new skills you otherwise might hardly have noticed.

Building a brain-training lifestyle

We hope that both you and your baby will find the specific games and activities we suggest in this book fun. They are based on what we know about how babies' intelligence develops, and if your baby does find them fun, then this in itself is pretty good evidence that they are good brain-building exercises.

Some other books on the market suggest that such games are some sort of fail-safe way of guaranteeing a higher IQ in just minutes of training a day. One bestseller on brain training suggests parents 'work' with their babies on these sorts of games 'for half an hour most days'. We would question both the science and the general attitude behind these sorts of recommendations.

We believe that the way you raise your children can make a big difference to their brain power. We doubt though that the big differences come from intense but brief and self-contained coaching sessions. There is no evidence to show that this sort of training works. Also, we don't think playing with your baby should be thought of as 'working' with them – that may well make both of you feel like giving up after a mere half-hour! Brain training goes on whenever you and your baby are enjoying being together: it's about fun, and it's about the way you live from hour to hour and minute to minute.

Interestingly, some research suggests that babies in 'underdeveloped' societies tend to reach the developmental milestones of the first year earlier than babies in developed countries. This suggests that there may be less-than-ideal things about the general ways in which we deal with our babies that more than cancel out the extra stimulation to be had from flash cards and expensive toys.

Babies spend *every waking hour* – and perhaps sleeping hours too – learning, and the way you can have the greatest effect is by giving your baby a whole brain-building lifestyle. How and where they eat, sleep, travel and just hang out, around the clock, will be the most crucial factors in how their brain develops. For that reason, we make lots of suggestions about how you might design a lifestyle that could help your baby learn.

How do I use this book?

The information and tips in this book are arranged very roughly in the order in which you will need them. You might want to read the whole book, or at least the early chapters, before your baby arrives. Then you can read, or re-read as a reminder, the later chapters as they become relevant to your baby's stage of development. You may notice that the age ranges covered by particular chapters overlap – 0 to three months, three to eight months, eight to 12 months, etc. This is meant to reflect roughly the way that babies develop. Not only do individual babies develop various individual skills at very different speeds, but they often move back and forward a bit, or change completely on one front while they stay very much at the same stage on another. As your baby grows, you will need to read not only the chapters specifically devoted to their particular stage of development, but also the chapters that come immediately before and after, as these develop and build on essential skills and knowledge in a way that helps you make progress along with your baby.

1

Preparing to take on the world's most highly skilled job

In this chapter you will learn:
- *how babies' brains grow and develop as they learn*
- *how you can influence the way your baby's intelligence develops*
- *how to create a healthy brain-building environment inside the womb*
- *how to prepare yourself for training your newborn baby.*

The technical bit: how your baby's brain develops *(skip if you have a science allergy)*

Bees can do some really clever things that most humans can't do. They can, for instance, do a special dance to tell their family exactly where a good source of nectar is. Many other animals also have other such special talents that seem way beyond us. So why do we think we are so smart?

One very big reason is that most animals are born with many of their most impressive skills. They don't really learn them, or if they do learn them, as some types of birds learn how to sing, the skills they are capable of learning are often quite specific. The amazing thing about human intelligence is that it allows us either to learn how to whistle like a blackbird or to invent a system of dance moves that would communicate the way to the next field of lavender (not that we've tried). Though other adaptable animals, such as rats, are also good learners, humans are the best learners on earth – and during childhood, we learn how to learn.

Some of our most impressive skills – for example, the ability to learn language – are most easily learned very young. Human babyhood and childhood is special – especially long, and especially important and exciting – because, instead of being born into the world with a whole batch of pre-programmed skills, human babies are born capable of doing almost nothing, but capable of *learning* to do almost anything.

It's natural to think of the brain as a sort of empty box for storing information, and of learning as a matter of piling information into the box. If that were the case, brain training would be a simple matter of feeding in information in a reasonable order as quickly as possible.

But the newborn baby's brain is not an empty box. It is slightly more like a powerful computer full of intricate circuits, with only minimal software installed. But it's not that much like a computer either, partly because the brain can 'soup' itself up in particular areas of functioning, all of its own accord. The unique way the brain grows is key to its amazing power, and to its amazing adaptability.

The brain is full of special cells, called neurons. Each neuron receives impulses through tiny hair-like structures called dendrites. The neuron passes the impulse on through a long cable-like structure called an axon. At the end of the axon, the impulse must leap a gap, called a synapse, to reach the dendrites of other neurons. To make this leap, the impulse relies on hormone-like chemicals called neurotransmitters. Thinking happens when impulses pass smoothly from neuron to neuron, onwards.

There are four important processes we know about that help this thinking process to develop.

1 At birth, each neuron has only fine, simple dendrites. These dendrites must grow stronger and branch out – just like an oak tree growing from a spindly sapling that has just a couple of twigs. The dendrites are biologically programmed to grow quickly during the earliest years of life, but their development is also determined by the impulses they receive. The more traffic each particular neuron receives, the stronger its dendrites grow, and the easier it is for impulses to leap the synaptic connections between that neuron and the next. Depending on the particular experiences it encounters, information highways through the brain begin to develop and widen, like paths through the

undergrowth, which gradually become beaten tracks and eventually roads, the more they are used.

2 For these information highways to form, the brain must also be bathed in the right balance of neurotransmitters to help information leap the synaptic gaps between the axon of one brain cell and the dendrites of others. The ratio of neurotransmitters in the brain is partly a matter of genetics, but it is also greatly affected by experience. For example, physical exercise and positive emotions produce a surge of various neurotransmitters that may help the brain work more quickly. Neurotransmitters strongly affect and are affected by mood and emotional state. Though we are not sure, it may be that the balance of neurotransmitters is one of the things that can most easily be shaped by a baby's environment.

3 At birth, the axons in your baby's brain are like badly insulated electrical cable. They become steadily better insulated with a fatty substance called myelin as baby grows, right on into early adulthood. This may be the process over which you, as a brain trainer, have least influence. On the other hand, a good supply of fatty acids in a baby's diet is needed for myelination – and that you can ensure. Loving contact has also been linked with increased myelin production.

4 The fourth, and most surprising, process in the growth of the brain is synaptic pruning. As some neurons, stimulated by use, produce more and more dendrite branches and synaptic connections with other neurons, brain cells and connections that are *not* used die away. This is a necessary process to help the smooth transmission of impulses along the more used information highways – so that information traffic does not take wrong turns down blind alleys. But it does mean that when it comes to brain development, it is really a matter of 'use it or lose it'.

The development of the brain is a very complex interaction between almost inevitable biological development, and learning and shaping through the environment – and, of course, the brain trainer is the key figure in that environment! Even as adults our brains can be radically, and literally, reshaped by our experience. In one well-known example, it was found that London cab drivers had extraordinarily well-developed parts of the brain responsible for navigation and spatial memory. This was not because they went into the job as good navigators, but because each time they figured out the quickest way around Green Park at five thirty in the afternoon, the neural connections in that part of the brain strengthened and branched out that bit more.

Baby's brains, though, are even more plastic, more mouldable, because a baby's body channels much more of its energy into super-fast brain development. And different areas of the brain seem to be biologically programmed to develop at different times.

The brain is very adaptable, and often the same task can be completed using quite different parts of the brain. But there seem to be areas of the brain specialized for particular functions. One of the best understood examples of this relates to language. The part of the brain used for language grows particularly quickly from six months through to early childhood – this is a critical period for language development. For this reason, it is much easier for children under ten to learn not only a first, but also a second language, than it is for teenagers or adults. On the other hand, if a child is not exposed to language during early childhood, the language parts of the brain may not be able to develop normally.

Childhood may be a formative period in other respects as well. Trauma and stress during childhood may permanently shape the brain and its balance and use of neurotransmitters in ways that will affect a child's adult temperament and mood.

There is a huge amount we have yet to discover about brain development and the role of the environment in shaping it. Critical periods and the death of unused brain cell connections sound rather alarming to any conscientious brain trainer, and it would be wonderful to have a full programme for the time-windows when each part of the brain could be worked on to greatest effect.

But the good news is that babies and young children seem very good at seeking out the kind of stimulation they need exactly when they need it. If your baby, overnight, seems to have started to want to do nothing but babble, clap, point and make animal noises with you, you can bet on it that the language and communication parts of their brain are having a growth spurt, and you don't need to worry that they are 'neglecting' their spatial skills. Let your baby lead you, and you can help your baby's brain grow into a teeming, diverse and luxurious rain forest of neural pathways.

What difference can you make? Genes and environment – and the stuff in between

It's not only parents who wonder whether it is nature or nurture that is the more important in determining how children turn out. Scientists have argued over the question for centuries too. Recently, we have begun to appreciate that the conundrum may not make sense. Many traits we inherit through our genes can only be expressed given the right environmental circumstances. Most of how we turn out is an interaction between our genes and our environment. So all pronouncements about the differing proportions of personality or intelligence that are determined by genes and environment, respectively, need to be taken with a very big pinch of salt.

Most parents, though, are surprised by how pre-programmed their baby does seem to be when it arrives. Siblings can seem radically different from one another from the minute they are born – and that's even though they actually share a whole lot of genes! Indeed, studies of identical twins (who share a full set of genes) that are brought up apart, suggest that about 40 per cent of the variation in the IQ scores of children is down to their genes. Interestingly, though, in studies of adult twins as much as 80 per cent of the variation in IQ scores seems to be down to genes.

The implication of this could be that genes may set a ceiling level for IQ and that in the course of time individuals are increasingly able to find ways of fulfilling their potential, overcoming deficiencies in the richness of their environments.

So does this mean that even your best parenting might only make a 20 per cent difference?

No – the picture is more complicated than that. Studies that have attempted to look particularly at children from deprived backgrounds suggest that genes may have a smaller role in determining their IQ scores than is the case among children brought up in more comfortable families. This suggests that genetic differences in intelligence only come fully into play if the environment is sufficiently supportive. However, we know from the example of Romanian orphanages and cases of criminal neglect that extreme negligence can lead to very severe developmental problems that cannot be rectified later on.

Of course, the most important element in determining the supportiveness of a child's environment is not the size of income to spend on toys, but the time and effort invested by parents. And studies also suggest that not only genes, but also the environment *before* birth – in the womb – may make a difference to eventual IQ. So you can start work even before your baby arrives!

The fact that the degree to which genes predict IQ grows with age – that people seem to overcome shortcomings in their environment to reach their full intellectual potential with time – suggests that your brain training efforts can really make a big difference, but perhaps not in the way you might imagine.

You might be thinking that baby brain-training means hard work for you and baby now, for the sake of a payoff much later: for example, a focus on early language skills might pave the way for a place on the board of directors at age 50.

Well you may indeed be able to make a substantial difference to your child's IQ score at age 50, and the big difference you can certainly make to how they do in primary school may indeed have knock-on effects on the whole of their career. But what is even more certain is that your brain training efforts will mean that your child doesn't have to wait decades to fulfil their full intellectual potential. You have it in your power to give their mind full play from day one. Science now suggests that we should see childhood not just as mental preparation for adulthood, but as a life stage with its own intellectual strengths. A leading psychologist has talked about a division in labour between adult and child intelligence – children do research and development, the blue-skies thinking, while adults do the less exciting work in marketing and production. With you as their brain trainer, your child can fulfil the extraordinary, fleeting potential of those wonderful early years while they last.

Brain training for babies is not about pain now for gain later – it's about ongoing fulfilment from square one.

Building a bright baby in the womb

A good environment *before* birth is strongly linked with mental health and intelligence. As well as following the standard cautions about foods and activities to avoid during pregnancy, here are some of the most important things you should consider.

AVOID ENVIRONMENTAL HAZARDS

Think carefully about whether your job exposes you to any dangerous chemicals or other hazards such as radiation or infective disease. Your employer should be able to have the level or risk assessed for you, if you have concerns. Take extra care out of work too – avoid hobbies or DIY projects that involve solvents and other chemicals. Be particularly careful stripping paint that may contain lead that you could pass on to your foetus. Avoid heavy traffic pollution if you can.

EXERCISE AND EAT HEALTHILY

Research shows that regular gentle exercise, such as swimming and walking, benefits foetal brain development. Exercise, along with a balanced diet, should also help you gain the optimal amount of weight during pregnancy, a factor that is also important for your baby's brain development.

DON'T TAKE ANY UNNECESSARY DRUGS

The effect of most drugs on unborn babies is unknown. Though research has suggested that some very common drugs, such as paracetamol and ibuprofen, are relatively safe, you should not take any drugs during pregnancy unless you really need to do so.

DON'T DRINK ALCOHOL

We know that high alcohol consumption can seriously damage the development of your baby's brain, leading to a common condition known as foetal alcohol syndrome. Given that alcohol can cross the placenta, it probably should not be part of your lifestyle while pregnant. The evidence so far has not found any risk from the occasional drink (one or two units a week), but we cannot yet be sure that even moderate drinking is always safe for all pregnant women.

DON'T SMOKE

Smoking seriously limits the flow of blood to baby's growing brain.

WATCH YOUR BLOOD PRESSURE

If your blood pressure is too high, the flow to your baby through the placenta is less efficient. Include beetroot juice and hibiscus tea in your diet; both have been shown to regulate blood pressure. Make sure you get enough calcium, and eat as much salt as you feel like.

TAKE FOLIC ACID OR FOLATE SUPPLEMENTS

Low levels of this B vitamin have been strongly linked not only with serious congenital disease, but also with hyperactivity and other developmental problems. You should ideally take a supplement from three months before you conceive to make certain you are getting enough. Eat folate-containing foods such as green leafy vegetables, wheat germ and orange juice.

TAKE FISH OIL SUPPLEMENTS – BUT NOT COD LIVER OIL

The modern diet is very low in the long-chain fatty acids so important for building a brain; so it makes sense to ensure that you have a good supply during pregnancy, especially from 18 weeks onwards when your baby's brain is growing fastest. Most of us do not eat much oily fish, but too much during pregnancy may put your baby at risk from heavy metal residues; and the farmed meat we eat is high in omega 6 but low in omega 3 fatty acids. Good fish oil supplements are a safe and effective way of increasing our intake of the latter. Avoid oil from fish liver, which may contain vitamin A, which has been shown to be a cause of birth defects. You should look for oil that has been 'molecularly distilled' for purity, is described as 'pharmaceutical grade', or that has passed national or international quality checks. You should look at the level of the two most important omega 3 fatty acids - EPA (Eicosapentaenoic Acid) and DHA (Docosahexaenoic Acid). There should be more of the former than of the latter, and while pregnant you should aim for an omega 3 total of 600 mg. Go for a supplement designed for pregnant women if you can find one with good levels of EPA and DHA.

AVOID LIQUORICE

One study showed that the IQ scores of children whose mothers ate a lot of liquorice during pregnancy were lower than those of mothers who did not. It may also raise blood pressure. If you drink herbal tea regularly, check that it does not contain liquorice – an increasingly common ingredient.

8

SUNBATHE SAFELY, OR TAKE VITAMIN D

Vitamin D insufficiency during pregnancy has been linked to various mental disorders. For example, babies born at the end of the winter are more likely to suffer from schizophrenia and MS. This is because sunlight is our main source of vitamin D. The angle of the sun's rays in Northern Europe between October and March (and also in the mornings and evenings) make it impossible for us to synthesize vitamin D. Clouds and sunblock also block the rays we need to make vitamin D. If you are pregnant during the summer months, you should be able to get most of the vitamin D you need from sunlight, without putting yourself at risk of skin cancer. Your skin only makes vitamin D for the first ten or 20 minutes of sun exposure – so you could take the opportunity to sunbathe for ten minutes during the middle of the day, each day. Alternatively, if you have little chance to get out and about, have a dark complexion, or are pregnant during the winter, you should take a vitamin D supplement. The government recommends 400IU a day, though many scientists believe this may not be nearly enough, and some suggest 1000–2000 IU. Pregnancy multi-vitamins often contain this higher amount.

RELAX

As a pregnant woman, you should take advantage of the fact that it's your duty as a parent to take it easy. Stress may be bad for the development of your baby's brain, and relaxation and happiness should have a positive effect. In an interesting piece of research, pregnant mothers listened to music through headphones. When they listened to music they liked, their foetuses moved around more, seemed to dance – even though the babies could not hear the music! If you find working during pregnancy stressful, you might think about beginning your leave early. Ask someone to give you massages, using relaxing, and blood pressure regulating essential oils such as lavender, bergamot and ylang-ylang, all safe during pregnancy. You might also try carrying a handkerchief or wearing a locket with some of your favourite essential oil in it, ready to sniff whenever you feel stressed. Research shows these fragrant measures really may help.

Insight

With so much ahead of her to think about, Brigid found relaxing during pregnancy much easier said than done. The best therapy was to go on lots of long walks in green places with chatty companions – excellent, soothing exercise for body and mind.

Unborn babies have big ears

Research shows that your foetus is listening and learning even in the womb. Mothers who read *The Cat in the Hat* out loud regularly to their bumps had babies who preferred the sound of that story to an unfamiliar one. Similarly, newborns were soothed by the sound of the credit music to soap operas that their mothers had watched regularly during pregnancy. Taking your cue from this research, you too could, before baby's birth, regularly read aloud a story or poem you would like to become a favourite later, or play music that you would like to become a naptime standby. Once your baby is born, it will be interesting to watch for signs of recognition and preference.

Training the baby trainer

Get ready – you are about to take on the most challenging job on earth – and if you're like most modern parents, you've had no training. You may not even know what kind of challenges lie ahead. New parents sometimes don't recognize the size of the challenge that lies ahead precisely because they lack training. Your baby will set you brainteasers a great deal harder than perfecting the wrap of a cloth nappy.

Why is it so common to hear mothers on maternity leave talk about vegetating at home with their babies, a turn of phrase that suggests that, lovely and cuddly though their babies may be, they offer no work for the brain? Maybe mothers feel they ought to sound self-deprecating, having spent time away from what is thought of as 'real' work. Our society is not good at understanding the hard work and skill that goes into caring well for babies. Be in no doubt – baby brain-training is not only one of the most important jobs on earth, it's also the most skilled and the most challenging. It may be possible to muddle through by the seat of your pants without taxing your intellectual powers too much, but to make parenting an art you have to put your whole mind to it. The development of the human brain is the most complex and intricate process on earth. Intervening positively in that process is life's most ambitious career path.

We want you to think of brain training as an art, as well as a science. We want to help you to aim high, and to take pride in your skills as they develop. Having spent time training both world-class university students on the one hand, and babies on the other, we would say that the babies offer far more of an intellectual challenge!

Practice makes perfect

One problem which most parents in our society face is that we don't have much contact with babies until we have our own. Historically speaking, this is a very unusual state of affairs. Research suggests that human mothers have always been happy to pass around their babies to trustworthy friends and relations for care and admiration. Many primates show great eagerness to hold the babies in their social group. Young females of various other species even seem as keen to nurse a doll as your average human seven-year-old.

This is not as surprising as it seems. Among many species, the offspring of parents who have had the most practice do best. It's easy to imagine that you learn skills and coping strategies with practice.

But much more than this is true: the brains of individuals who have had practice caring for infants are actually altered in the long term by that experience. The same sort of brain changes encouraging nurturing behaviour also happen during pregnancy – not only in a woman's brain, but in her partner's too, if they are around. And these changes will be amplified by previous time spent around babies. Again, this is not just a matter of conscious learning. Even experiences you do not remember may have permanently changed your brain. If you have a younger sibling, for example, your brain may be better prepared to look after your own babies.

If you have any opportunities to hang around babies before or during your pregnancy, do take them. It will help your brain shape up for the challenge.

Mindful parenting

One reason that the work involved in raising a baby is not always appreciated – and that looking after a baby can feel really hard and yet still be described as undemanding – is that it is a very special kind of work. Being good at it doesn't involve the sort of speed and efficiency needed to get the garden weeded or the lawn mown or the house cleaned. It doesn't involve the same abstracted mental concentration as writing a book. But, nevertheless, it does need all your energy, all your skill, and all your mind. In order to work hard for your baby, **you need to engage with them in each particular instant – you have to focus on, be fully present for, each unique moment in the development of your individual child**. This engagement may not come easily, but when it does come it will make your parenting better and your job easier and more satisfying.

In recent years, psychologists have demonstrated the benefits of practicing this special kind of awareness, which has roots in Zen Buddhism, and is now often called 'mindfulness'. There's good evidence that mindfulness can alleviate psychological problems such as anxiety and depression, and boost mental wellbeing. It can help with periods of change and adjustment, and is particularly good training for the sort of mental engagement it takes to be a baby brain trainer. Indeed, several books have been published about mindfulness and parenting. You might want to start to practise during pregnancy.

Some people practise mindfulness through meditation, but you can also practise as you go about your business. You are aiming for a state of accepting awareness of the present moment. As you brush your teeth, looking out the window, **take in what you feel and what you see –** the taste of the toothpaste, the bristles on your gums, the increasing slipperiness of the brush handle – the colour of the clouds, the speed they move – the angle of shadows, the transparency of the leaves. **Do not fight to empty your thoughts, but notice the thoughts, plans, judgements, and worries going through your mind.** Don't identify with them, but stand back from them and let them pass, rather than being rolled up and swept away by them. **Try to take up a noticing position *between* your awareness of outside things and inside thoughts.**

Immerse yourself in the present moment as often as you can throughout the day. Make an effort to adopt this mental attitude each time you do daily tasks such as brushing your hair, climbing the stairs, washing up – until the tasks automatically bring you back to mindfulness.

Trying to be aware of your own states of awareness, relaxation and attention will in itself help you understand and get on top of the hard work of parenting, and will make sure you make the most of each unique moment in the exciting process of training your amazing baby's brain.

Learn how to do baby research

Modern parents are cut off from a lot of the practice with babies, and a lot of the support structures that traditional village societies, for example, would have given them. In societies of that kind, there are very complex and detailed traditions of baby care that are shared by everyone. New parents just need to follow rules with which they are already very familiar. As a modern parent, on the other hand, you may be all too aware that there's a very wide range of parenting practices out there, and you're not fully initiated into any of them. In some ways this is a hassle. But in others it is an opportunity. The internet, along with the myriad of parenting books available to you, opens up a huge range of paths through every dimension of parenting. Somewhere out there on the web is the perfect solution to each parenting problem, tailored to the peculiarities of you and of your baby. Before your baby is born, **check out baby shops, parenting forums, information sites and bookshops.** See *Further resources* at the end of this book for good places to start.

Seek out brain-building activities

Once baby arrives, it may be hard to find the time to discover what's going on in the area where you live. So, in advance, **make yourself a list of the times and places of classes you might like to try out** – baby swimming, baby massage, parent and child groups. Also, **give a bit of thought to the sort of places you'd like to go to with your new baby.** You may not be able to do your usual ten-mile hikes, all-day shopping expeditions, or trips to the cinema for a while, but you and your baby will enjoy getting out. For the first six months, even very short expeditions will be great for brain training. Look out for the park with lots of dogs, the waste ground by the supermarket car-park that is full of dandelion clocks, the pet shop that stocks tropical fish, the pier, and the building site with exciting cranes and diggers.

Tailoring your expectations

Before the birth, almost the only thing you can be certain of about your baby's temperament, habits and personality is that they will surprise you. After ten years of parenting, you will still be regularly amazed by the particularity of your child, the many ways in which they differ quite radically from any other child you know. To be a good brain trainer, you will need to be alert to, and very accepting of, this particularity. Even when it comes to something as basic as sleep, babies show amazing differences. Newborns sleep on average somewhere between eight and 20 hours out of every 24. If your newborn (like one of mine) sleeps eight hours, and your best friend has a baby on 20 hours, you may think you are doing something very wrong, or that there is something wrong with your baby. Much more likely is that your baby is just like that, and trying to get 20 hours of sleep out of them will just lead to boredom and tears. So before your baby is born, try to assume almost nothing. It doesn't matter what the babies do in films or in catalogues, your baby has not seen these and does not care about fitting in. They may never let you put them in a pushchair. They may refuse to lie down to have their nappy changed. They may only be able to get to sleep if you hold them in one arm and a pot plant in the other. Your baby may hate the nursery but find it really interesting to hang out in the broom cupboard. As parents, it is 'ours not to reason why'. Just go with it. As long as your baby is healthy and safe, all other peculiarities are there just to be wondered at and, as far as possible, catered to. Baby will chose the kind of training they need.

Enjoying your baby

The bottom line is – whenever you and your baby are happy together, enjoying each other, you'll be training baby's brain. This book is aimed at helping you achieve that simple goal. Your baby's brain will develop faster than you can imagine – by the time they are six months old, you will hardly be able to believe all they have achieved in half a year. Go away for two days, and you'll find they have changed a little since you've been away. And you won't want to miss any of it. Even while you will be constantly excited about your baby's progress towards the next milestone, you will also wish they could be exactly the delicious, entrancing age they are now, forever. Babies teach us an important lesson about seizing the moment. Enjoy your baby, and let them enjoy you.

Activity: Plant a baby garden

Research shows that time spent in the natural world has marvellous effects on brain activity in adults. The babies in our family love nothing as much as being outside, and seem to find it every bit as relaxing as the adults in research studies. By exposing your baby's brain to the sights, smells, tastes, sounds and feelings of nature, you will build synaptic connections that may help them enjoy the therapeutic pleasures of the natural world as an adult.

In the first year, your baby will be more interested in what is small-scale and up close than extensive panoramas. Whether you have a big garden or just a window box, you can have a bit of it that is just for them to enjoy; somewhere where they can be totally safe to mess about and to smell, feel, and taste natural things.

Plant this garden in clean compost or soil. Make sure cats and dogs can't foul the area. Once all your plants are growing, you could cover the soil with a layer of play sand, which will also put off the slugs.

Here are five of the best plants for your baby to enjoy. All are small, easy to grow in almost any position, completely non-toxic, and will appeal to more than one of your baby's senses.

Wild or alpine strawberries (*fragaria vesca*) – pretty white flowers that are followed by tiny red fruit through the

(*Contd*)

summer. These are an ideal first food for baby, and by nine months they may be picking their own! Easiest to buy as small plants at garden centres.

Pot marigold (*calendula*) – lovely golden flowers in summer, with petals that are delicious to eat and fun to pick off. One of the easiest flowers to grow from seed.

Nasturtiums (*tropaeolum*) – beautiful flowers in later summer, with both flowers and leaves having a spicy taste that babies love. Stick a seed into the ground at any time of year and you will almost certainly end up with a good crop of flowers! The plants will climb, or hang down from a pot or window box.

Pansies or violets (*viola*) – the whole viola family has edible, as well as beautiful, flowers, and they are easy to pick up at garden centres. Different varieties flower at different times, so you can enjoy them throughout the year.

Double daisies (*bellis perennis flore plen*) – edible and easy to grow. Your baby will like the buds as well as the open flowers.

YOUR TURN

▶ Think carefully about your lifestyle – make sure you are not exposed to environmental toxins or hazards. The environment inside the womb is crucially important for your baby's brain development.

▶ Review your diet – remember that what a pregnant mother eats and drinks may be at least as, or more, significant for her child's cognitive development than what the child eats during childhood. Eat whole foods and fruit and vegetables, and avoid white flour, sugar and hydrogenated fats.

▶ Consider supplements – there is evidence that supplements of vitamin D, folic acid, and fish oil, may aid your baby's brain development.

▶ Relax – too much stress may be bad for your developing baby's brain.

▶ Work on your mental habits, and consider practising mindfulness. A healthy psychological attitude will make you a better brain trainer.

▶ Manage your expectations – think ahead to what life will be like with a new baby, but keep your mind open, ready to be surprised and delighted by your unique new baby.

▶ Develop your baby research skills – explore books and websites with information and conversation about babies and parenting.

2

....

Your talented newborn: brain training from 0 to three months

In this chapter you will learn:
- *what the world is like for a newborn baby*
- *how to help regulate your newborn's psychological states*
- *how to help your newborn makes sense of new impressions*
- *how to create a stimulating newborn environment.*

During the first weeks of life, your baby will be working on the very basics. Small as they are, your baby has a huge challenge ahead of them.

They will be getting used to feeding, digesting and breathing, instead of taking in all their nourishment through the umbilical chord. They will be learning to sleep in the noisy outdoor world of night and day. They will be getting used to having space to move their limbs again. They will be practising seeing, hearing, tasting, smelling and touching, and beginning to unravel the tangle of new impressions reaching them through their senses. And finally, your baby's emotional system will be attempting to deal with these huge biological changes and floods of new information.

Baby was recently, in a way, just a part of their mother's body. And now, although they are outside in the world, they need to stay closer than close: their body, and also their mind, cannot develop without your constant help. They need not only to be fed and kept warm by their carers, but also to adjust their own psychological state by their mother keeping close to them.

When your baby was born, naked and damp, they needed to be held close to your body so that your warmth could flow into them: the feel of your skin regulated the temperature of your baby's. In just the same way, during the early months, being close to an emotionally and psychologically balanced adult who is in tune with them will help them ride the sea of new impressions flooding their mind and body.

Your most important job as a brain trainer during these early months is to help your baby to cope with the waves of feeling that will sweep over them as they get used to the world. To do this, you need to **stay physically and psychologically close.**

You can also make a difference by making sure their environment is rich in sights, smells and sounds of the kind most accessible to their developing senses. Once you have learned about the way they experience the world, you can help them begin to make sense of all this new experience.

Your baby is training YOUR brain

Research shows that many areas of the brains of new mothers grow bigger after their babies are born. The more you dote on your new baby, the more your brain is likely to grow! There is also science to suggest that parenthood in humans and other animals may boost intelligence in a whole range of areas such as perception, efficiency, resilience, motivation and emotional intelligence.

The first hours of life

Much of what your newborn can do at birth is a matter of *reflex*. They are born programmed to react in certain ways to certain kinds of stimulus experience. Touch your baby's cheek and they will 'root', that is, open their mouth to suckle, on the side you've touched. Move them too quickly and they will fling out their arms to save themselves from a fall. Give them a finger and they will grip it tightly. Your baby will lose these reflexes sometime during the first six months, but learn how to do some of the same things voluntarily, instead. Your newborn can also do amazing things like hold their breath and swim underwater. Once they lose this reflex, it may take them years to learn the same skill voluntarily. If you stand your baby on a flat surface, they will make stepping motions. Again, this reflex will fade, but not much later they will learn to take steps of their own volition. In general, more intelligent, more adaptable animals, like human beings, depend more on learned skills and less on reflexes. The skills we learn can be specifically tailored to the environment in which we find ourselves.

WHAT YOUR NEWBORN SEES

Your newborn has quite bad eyesight, finding it hard to focus on things further away than eight inches or so. They focus best at about the distance your face is from theirs if they are suckling. Your face is what they are born to look at, and staring long and hard into your eyes is one of the first skills your baby learns. You may notice that their gaze becomes more focused and longer lasting over the course of the first six weeks. **Try tilting your head as your baby stares into your eyes** – they may tilt theirs too!

A nineteenth century psychologist, William James, speculated that the experience of a newborn must be 'a booming, buzzing confusion'. That may or may not be so, but newborns are certainly programmed to know how to start sorting things out. One of the first things your newborn will be working on is figuring out which parts of the pattern they see before their eyes belong together. They can't begin to categorize and learn about things until they know where one thing ends and another begins.

A South American legend tells that the native people were terrified when they saw their first mounted horseman, because they thought man and horse were part of the same monstrous animal. This is the kind of confusion faced by babies, a confusion difficult to get over if you lack background experience. Because they do lack experience, young babies would not be at all surprised to come across a real version of *Alice in Wonderland*'s Cheshire Cat, whose smile appears and disappears without the rest of the animal it belongs to. Is the television remote part of the tablecloth? Is the tablecloth part of the floor visible below it?

It's because they are so interested in this problem that babies of this age are visually drawn most of all to two things: edges and movement. When your newborn looks at you, you may notice them systematically scanning the edges of your face. If you put on a hair scarf that changes your face's outline, they may not recognize you.

Babies rightly expect that areas of strong contrast may well mark the edges of things. Many animals process what they see this way – the bold stripes on a zebra work as camouflage because they break up the real shape of the animal.

To help baby build on this fascination with edges, **choose toys, baby equipment and nursery decorations with clear lines and bold colour contrasts**. The soft-focus pictures in pastel shades you see on some baby gear certainly won't be your newborn's favourite things to look at.

Babies love slow ceiling fans with dark blades. These combine their passion for contrast with their passion for movement. Again, movement is key to identifying individual things within a field of vision. Usually, if something moves all at once, that means it is all one thing – that's why it would be reasonable to imagine a mounted horseman and his steed to be just one animal.

Help baby practise picking out objects from their background, and tracking their movement, by moving your hand, with fingers wiggling, or holding a brightly coloured object, from one side to another in an arch about a foot in front of your baby's face. You will be able to see them becoming more and more adept at tracking each day. You might also try shaking a noisy object like a bell or rattle, first on one side and then on the other. Again, babies tend to look towards a sound from birth – they expect to be able to see something to go with an interesting noise. As your baby becomes more alert and coordinated, they will look the right way, towards the source of sound, most of the time.

Newborns prefer more complex patterns to simpler ones, and prefer patterns that look like faces to ones that do not. Your baby is born to look longer at human faces than anything else. They notice different expressions, conveying different emotions, and may even be able to imitate them. Within days, they will prefer to look at their own mother's face than a stranger's. In one interesting experiment, newborns were shown two patterns of dancing lights, one created by fixing lights to the limbs of dancers in the dark, the other created at random. Babies preferred to look at the 'human' light show.

Babies are born preferring to look at human faces and human movement because learning about and bonding with other human beings is the rock on which everything else they learn is built. In fact, they find it difficult to learn much else at all unless they have a good feel for other people. Remember this. No matter how brain boosting your baby's mobile, your face is even more brain-boosting. It may be that the earliest experiences snowball, so that a baby who gets used to looking at faces in the first days and weeks of life is already on the road to sociability, good people skills, and boosted intelligence. **During the early weeks, try to make sure there is a loving face within sight whenever baby looks for one – and let them gaze at it until they choose to look away.**

Can your newborn copy your expressions?

Babies are born with the ability to imitate expressions – which is a more amazing fact than you might think. It suggests that they innately link the way your face looks on the outside to the way they feel on the inside. At a time when your baby is well rested and alert, pull some faces and see if they follow. The best faces to get a reaction are a sticking out tongue and a wide-open round mouth, a wide letter-box mouth or pursed lips. Give your baby a long time to manage their imitation – at least a couple of minutes.

Sometimes your baby's imitation may be very subtle. Scientists studying imitation have used this trick to determine whether babies were really imitating: Have someone else stand behind you so that they can't see your face, but can see baby's. Can they see your face 'mirrored' in your baby's, and so guess what expression you are pulling?

WHAT YOUR NEWBORN HEARS

By the time they are born, babies' hearing has already been well developed for several weeks. Newborns cannot hear sounds as quiet as adults can, but they can discriminate very well among different kinds of sound. They are born with a preference for their mother's voice, probably because they hear it well inside the womb. They find very low and very high-pitched noises disturbing, preferring moderately low-pitched sounds. Their hearing seems designed to pick out human noises – they enjoy the sound of speech, and from very early can be observed 'dancing' to its rhythm. They prefer any music to noise, but show a marked preference for vocal over instrumental tunes. Don't expect your baby to be amused by the muffled rattle made by most of the cloth-covered ankle or wrist rattles on the market – their hearing is not sharp enough to catch such a quiet sound.

Get into the habit of talking and singing to your baby from the very beginning – your voice is their favourite sound. It doesn't matter if you feel silly – talking to your baby is the second most important thing (after loving them) that you can do for their brain development.

Does your newborn recognize English?

Babies learn to distinguish the sound of their native language before or very soon after birth. If you have a second language, try switching to that suddenly in the middle of talking to your baby, or to your partner within the hearing of your baby. Does your baby react in any way? Do they gain or lose interest? Do they stop cooing to hear what's going on?

If you do have a second language, speak it around your baby often – the sooner they hear those different language noises and feels familiar with them, the better.

WHAT YOUR NEWBORN SMELLS

Newborns have an amazing sensitivity to smell, and as a brain trainer you need to be aware of this. At birth, newborns use smell to make sense of their world. Straight after emerging, a newborn baby, still wet with amniotic fluid, can wiggle towards its mother's breast to suckle, and as they do so, they leave a trail of scent that they can use later on, whenever they need to come back to the breast. Their saliva, also, contains smells that they can recognize – when your baby sucks and drools on you, they are marking you as their own! In hours, your baby will recognize your smell, particularly the smell of your milk – and will prefer to face towards one of your breast pads than a stranger's.

There is still a lot we don't understand about smell, but scientists are constantly discovering new and amazing ways in which scent triggers biological processes and psychological reactions. Until we know more about smell, we should be very cautious not to disrupt the way our babies experience it. If you can resist having an all-body shower straight after your baby is born, do – try to leave your baby with the familiar smell of amniotic fluid splashed around their new home in your arms, (though don't worry if this isn't possible). And **take it easy on the showers for the first few days** at home – let your baby learn your smell, being particularly careful not to wash and wipe off their drool every time they mark you with it. You and everyone around a new baby should **avoid strong perfume and deodorant** for as long as possible. **Switch to a natural washing powder** that doesn't contain artificial fragrances, avoid fabric conditioner, and banish the air-freshener. Even strong essential oils should be avoided in the early days. There is a theoretical risk that such strong smells might not only interfere with the scent communication between your new baby and you, but might even send 'wrong' messages that could disrupt their hormonal system.

You'll be amazed how sensitive your own sense of smell is when it comes to your new baby – you will probably be able to tell by scent if someone outside your closest circle has been holding them. Some mothers find it very disturbing if the smell of their newborn is masked by someone else's aftershave. It's good to become familiar with your baby's smell – **apply your nose to the top of their head and breathe deeply!**

Sucking

At birth and for a long while afterwards, your baby constantly uses their mouth to explore. Because they need to be able to suckle from the word go, they are born with very good connections between their mouth and brain. There is more myelin, the grease that helps information to travel, along the connections between their mouth and brain than there is on the connections to other parts of their body. Take advantage of this by giving your baby some interesting mouth experiences. **Touch their cheeks, and see how they root around for a nipple to suck. Try different sorts of touch on their cheeks and see how they respond. Then try touching your baby's lips with (clean!) objects of different textures. Put your finger to their lips – do they suck it as though it were a nipple?** As the weeks go by they will get better at telling the difference. Soon your baby will start to lick, as well as suck – a new way of exploring with their mouth.

Get in touch

For the first few days at home, do not envelop baby from head to toe in a babygro, but wrap one side of them in a warm blanket while you hold the other against your own naked skin (unbutton your shirt a bit, pull up your top, or even better, wear a bikini top, if the house is warm enough). Research shows that carrying and skin-to-skin contact helps premature babies grow, and the same may be true of full-term infants. Don't feel your baby must be fully dressed at all times – babygros and hats leave too little skin available to touch, and few of our houses are cold enough to make them essential. When they are against your bare skin, your baby's body temperature will be regulated by yours.

Make a habit of maintaining skin-to-skin contact whenever you can, especially if you are not able to breast feed. Whichever way you feed your baby, stroke them all over with your free hand when you do.

Touching and stroking releases oxytocin – which promotes relaxation and bonding – and prolactin, which is important in the production of myelin, the brain grease that gets brainwaves moving smoothly.

Get into the habit of feeling your baby's lovely skin – their velvety head, silky palms and soles, their peachy back and arms and rubbery legs. Your loving touch will communicate your affection, and, as we will see, feeling such affection helps their brain grow.

One of the first things your baby will learn is the feeling of their own body. In the early days, they will develop a mental map of their physical self from the inside out. To help your baby 'map' their body, run your hands over their skin from top to toe when you change them. Gently cycle and shake their arms and legs.

If you want to take touch further, you might also try baby massage, but if you or baby is happier with a less structured, more on-going touch regime, that's fine too. Just make sure you keep in touch…

Activity: baby massage

There's good evidence to support the benefits of massage for both babies and older children. For example, premature babies who were massaged gained almost 50 per cent more weight, were more active and alert, and were able to leave the hospital earlier than babies who were not. Baby massage has also been shown to strengthen the bond between mothers suffering from postnatal depression and their babies. None of this is surprising: because massage encourages skin-to skin contact, and stimulating touch, eye-contact and engagement, between baby and massager, it ticks all the boxes.

You may want to attend a baby massage class, which would be an outing for yourself and your baby. But there is no evidence to suggest that the benefits of massage come from specialized tricks of the trade. If you prefer to teach yourself, that should be fine. Be very gentle, follow your instincts, and, if you would like some ideas, use this basic guide:

Choose a time of day and a moment when your baby is relaxed and alert, but not too active – wild kicking can make massage difficult!

Your room needs to be quite warm, to help baby relax. Make sure your hands, your oils, and the surface for baby to lie on are all warm. Avoid overhead lights that dazzle baby and make it hard for them to focus on your face. Sit on the floor or the bed, put a towel under baby and lay them on their back on your lap. Put on soothing music if you like, but nothing with lyrics that could distract you from talking to baby.

Massage oils: You should only use natural oils without fragrance: Grapeseed oil or olive oil are good choices.

Be ready to give up if baby is in the wrong mood. You never can tell until you start. But do try again later – they could well be keen another time.

(Contd)

Work your way down baby's body.

1 You don't need oil for this first stage. Cup the back of baby's head in your hands – feel its lovely shape, and imagine the amazing activity going on in there! Begin by making tiny circles on your baby's head with your fingertips. Then smooth your baby's forehead – first outwards from the centre, and then downward toward the nose (watch the skin wrinkle as though they were a little pug dog). Then, using one or two fingers, make small circles around the hinge of the jaw, just in front of the ears.

2 Warm some oil in your hands and stroke your baby's chest outwards from the centre, one hand in each direction. Some massagers suggest you imagine you are drawing a big heart. Repeat several times.

3 Roll each arm between your palms, working down from the shoulder to the wrist. Enjoy the feel of the chub! Repeat a few times. On the final time, when you reach the hand, gently uncurl each finger and give it a gentle roll, then stroke the palm with your thumbs.

4 Gently massage that tummy with your flat hand, moving in a clockwise direction.

5 Roll each leg between your two hands as you did with the arms. Then grasp baby's thigh gently between thumb and fingers, and slowly slide your hand down toward the foot, as though you were easing out a ball of tension stuck in a tube.

6 Use the balls of your thumbs to press firmly all over the soles of baby's feet, including the balls of the toes. Always keep the ankles supported.

7 Stroke your baby's back. First across, then back and forth, working your way up from baby's bottom to the neck and back down again, then in long lines from shoulders to feet. Spread your fingers apart to make a comb. Firmly comb down from the top of baby's spine to their bottom. Gradually lighten the pressure until you are barely touching. Your baby will be able to anticipate the end of the routine.

Setting up a stimulating newborn environment

Nursery furniture and decorations are often poorly designed to appeal to young babies. Newborns are just not into all those washed out shades. Many are not even that interested in soft toys. In fact, most won't buy the idea of a nursery at all. Hanging around for a large part of the day in one room is seriously boring, especially if that room does not contain interesting things like sinks, vacuum cleaners, siblings, or you. Baby wants to be where you are, and wants you to move around as much as possible. So instead of making one room babyish all over, you might think about putting something to catch baby's eyes in each of the rooms you spend time in yourself.

FIRST MOBILES

Many books designed to build baby's brain power give ideas for mobiles – but we hesitate to do so. We hesitate because good brain trainers do not give their babies too much opportunity to stare at mobiles. So let's get it straight: the most stimulating mobile imaginable is absolutely no substitute for being on the move with you.

But sometimes baby will have to stay still – while you're changing their nappy, or maybe while you put on the food. They are more likely to tolerate this if you make the parking spots for these times particularly exciting. You may not want to invest too much time and money in decorating these areas though – babies tend eventually to get sick even of the best displays, and they will like you to change the scene every few weeks. Here are a couple of ideas that will take minutes and cost pennies.

TISSUE PAPER STREAMERS

Cut black, red, dark green or dark blue tissue paper into long strips, about four inches wide. Then fold up each strip like a concertina, so that each strip ends up as a four-inch square.

Cut bold shapes into the raw unfolded edges of each square. Cut curves on some, and sharp angles on others. When you unfold the paper, you should have long zigzag and curvy wave-shaped streamers.

Stick these to the ceiling above your changing table, or wherever else baby has to spend time on their back, so that they dangle out of their reach, but within their short field of vision. Cut or stick together the streamers to achieve the right length.

When you open a window or door, the streamers should move and rustle in the draught. If the air is still, you puff at them. Baby will love to see them move, especially if your puffing also makes an exciting noise!

At the beginning you will be able to lift your baby up and let them bat, kick or even scrunch the tissue paper. They will love this! Soon though they will get too good at grabbing, and will have those streamers on the way to their mouth, which is not a good idea, as the dye will run if they suck it. Snatch the paper away from your baby, and uncurl those little fingers from around the scrap left in the tiny fist. Time to take down the streamers and try something else.

CARD SPIRALS

Cut out a circle of darkly coloured thin card, somewhere around six inches to a foot in diameter. You could use boldly coloured paper plates, if you have any.

Then, starting at the edge cut a strip about an inch wide, spiralling in towards the centre. When you have finished, the card should hang down like a spring.

You can do the same thing with square, triangular, or even star or flower shaped card, to vary the effect.

How you hang your spirals will depend on the height of the ceiling and the place baby is to sit or lie. They should be within sight, but not close enough to grab. Either thread string through the centre of each spiral, attaching the string end to the ceiling, or attach the spirals directly onto the ceiling. Each way of hanging will give a different effect.

Give the spirals a gentle tug and they will bounce to baby's delight, especially if you say 'boioioing'!

LEAF CANOPY

Collect a variety of big, bold-shaped leaves such as you get from ferns, maples and oaks, and press them between the pages of a dictionary or other large book – if you don't want to mark the pages, use sheets of tissue paper on each side of the leaves. Stuff the book back into a full bookshelf, or pile other books on top to increase the pressure. You'll need to leave them for a week or more. When they are good and flat, glue them onto a big sheet of white paper or card – plain wallpaper works well. Stick it either to the ceiling or wall of a room where baby spends a lot of time. They will love the sharp contrasts and the bold, natural shapes of the leaves.

OTHER QUICK TIPS

If you have a chess-board, get it out and stick it somewhere in sight; babies love the chequered pattern. You might also try drawing big simple faces onto card or white paper plates, using thick black marker. Research shows you should include a hairline, chin, eyes and mouth if baby is to recognize it as a face. Brightly coloured real or artificial flowers are a hit with some newborns, giant red and black poppies best of all.

Look out for bold, colourful educational posters, even if they are much too advanced for your newborn to learn from directly. Alphabet friezes, for example, usually have pictures of common items to point out and talk about to baby. Remember that when choosing material for brain training, you need to consider what will stimulate *you*, the budding brain trainer, to talk to and play with your baby, just as much as what will stimulate your baby directly.

Crying

Some babies cry more than others. The differences usually emerge after the first two or three weeks. If your newborn cries for a few hours a day, on most days, for weeks on end, then they may be classified as having colic. The significance of this classification is hazy – we don't really know what causes colic, or even whether there is a common cause behind the distress of all babies who cry a lot. Given this lack of understanding, there is no need to worry about whether your baby's crying is or is not caused by colic, or to worry about the crying itself. There is no evidence to suggest colicky babies do less well in any way later in life. Indeed, some babies seem to cry because they are so intensely engaged with their environment, and so desperate to get on top of it.

On the other hand, you shouldn't be too resigned. When your baby is crying, they are not happy, and they are not learning. And you will also be keen to spare the family the distress of these episodes. It may turn out that you can't stop the crying, but it is worth pulling out all stops to help them. Each baby is different, and you should try as many strategies as you can. Here are a few tricks with a good track record.

To avoid the crying:

- ▶ **Try probiotics.** Research shows that the gut flora of colicky babies is distinctive, and some studies have shown that friendly bacteria reduce crying. There are, on the market, probiotics specifically designed for babies.
- ▶ **Reduce background stimulation levels.** Some babies cope less well with noisy, bustling environments than others. If you notice baby is more likely to cry on days when there are lots of people around, the television blaring, or you're in a rush to do errands, try sheltering baby from the bustle for a few days and see if that helps. This may be easier said than done, or course. Colic does seem commoner among second babies, which may be because it's harder for parents to keep a lid on background rumpus. The time of the evening meal, when parents have to cook and their big sibling is cranky with hunger, can be tricky for second-born children. Try a radical rejigging of your schedule. Could you eat at a different time, or prepare the meal in advance to eat later?
- ▶ **Try using a baby carrier.** Babies who are carried a lot, cry less. Being in close contact with a calm adult body may regulate stress chemicals in your baby's body so that crying is avoided.
- ▶ **Pre-empt the episodes.** Some babies cry at a predictable time each day, often in the evening. If so, half an hour before cry time, take baby to a dimly lit, quiet, warm room and strip them down to their nappy. Hold them skin-to-skin against your own naked body, and rock them and sing to them in whatever way they like best. Your smell and the feel of your skin will have powerful calming effects.
- ▶ **Make sure baby is not bored.** Even very young babies can get frustrated if they have to spend too long in the same place, position, or at the same activity. This need for variety, in a baby who is only three to six weeks old, can take parents by surprise. Some babies want you to ring the changes all day long. Try

spending time in different rooms of the house, holding baby in a wider variety of positions, playing different music, walking around for a while – anything to vary the stimulation.

> **Insight**
>
> Tass was slightly colicky. You could stop his crying by rolling your tongue to make a high-pitched purring sound near his ear. He also quietened to rattling noises. He couldn't hear toy rattles over his own roaring, but heavy pills or gravel in tins worked like magic.

Once the roaring has started:

- ▶ **Try soothing sounds.** Babies are very individual in their responses to noise. Vacuum cleaners or washing machines are old favourites. If you search the web you will find sites with samples of hundreds of different sounds, from babbling brooks, to wind in the trees, to rush hour traffic. One of these may do the trick.
- ▶ **Go outside.** Research shows that being outside, even for a short time, lowers stress levels in adults, and it seems to work for babies too. Even if it's dark and rainy outside, baby may cheer up with a breath of fresh air. A sharp breeze may distract them from their misery. Hold them very close, inside your own coat, to keep them warm.
- ▶ **Try a bath.** For some babies this will be a terrible idea, but others find it soothing. Try it once and you will know which kind you have! The room needs to be warm, your towel should be warm, and the water temperature should be warm but not hot. Don't use essential oils in the water for young babies: plain water is fine.
- ▶ **Try different kinds of rocking.** Research shows that, on average, babies are most soothed by rocking from side to side at about the speed of a heart beat. But babies vary greatly. Brigid's elder child, Ide, was soothed by very rhythmic, strong rocking, with firm pats on the back: we're talking more Nirvana than *Eine Kleine Nachtmusik*. Tass, baby number two, likes very slow, gentle swaying to laid-back jazz. Try out different holds. Many babies dislike lying in your arms in the classic baby-rocking position. Try facing baby over your shoulder in a 'winding' position, or upright and facing forward with their back against your body, or lying along your forearm, legs dangling down at your elbow, and your

hand under their chin. However you rock, take great care that baby's neck and head are fully supported and not jolted around.

▶ **Try a pram ride.** If coasting along on tarmac doesn't work, try going over bumps, or rolling to and fro over a manhole cover.

▶ **Never stop trying new strategies.** There may be a solution out there for the finding.

Remember your roots

Baby 'enrichment' products and programmes are often sold using the evidence of research on mice, which showed better brain development in those who had lots of especially stimulating toys added to their cages.

The fact that isn't usually mentioned is that even the mice with the enriched cages still had very poorly developed brains compared to mice living out in their natural habitat in the woods.

When deciding how to live with your baby and how to nurture their brain, bear in mind the fact that humans developed their amazing intelligence at a time when we lived roaming outdoor lives in groups of around 20 hunter-gatherers, and that human beings all lived that way for 190,000 years, until we slowly started to do things differently, a paltry 10,000 years ago.

This doesn't mean you should try to give your baby the life of a hunter-gatherer baby – I'm sure they are quite happy not to be at risk of being eaten by hyenas, thank you very much. Modernity offers huge, wonderful advantages and opportunities. But be wary of letting your child lead an existence completely cut off from the outdoors, and from the way we evolved to live, eat and sleep. If a friend or a book advises you, for example, that 'it is essential that baby learns to sleep in their own room by age one', you can be a little sceptical. Inventions as new as designated baby bedrooms are unlikely to be vital to your child's brain development. Unless we have good evidence that a particular practice is one of the unqualified goods of modernity, feel free to reject it.

Newborn smiles

You can expect your baby to start smiling at you at around six weeks of age. It's wonderful – keep courting those smiles until your cheek muscles ache! Smiling, and the laughing that begins a few weeks later, along with long gazes into your eyes, are your baby's first social advances. You can make a difference by encouraging them to smile, and being there to smile back as much of the time as you can. The more often you smile and laugh and show your delight, rewarding their efforts, the more often they will smile and laugh and brighten your day. Set your relationship with your baby off on a virtuous spiral of sociability and affection.

YOUR TURN

▶ Learn about how your newborn experiences the world, and try to see things through their eyes as you organize their life.

▶ Start building your baby's people skills. Make sure there is always a loving face for your newborn to stare at, for as long as they like.

▶ Let your newborn learn to trust you. Take pride in the speed and commitment with which you respond to your baby's cry.

▶ Spend some time in skin-to-skin contact with your baby.

▶ Work on soothing techniques to calm your baby when they are crying or tense. Be inventive and keep honing your skills.

▶ Try baby massage.

▶ Get used to talking to your baby as much as you can.

▶ Enhance the environment at home to stimulate your newborn's senses.

▶ When they are awake, don't leave your baby in their cot. Make sure they are up and about watching the action. Your baby is training YOUR brain.

3

All you need is love: the relationships behind intelligence

In this chapter you will learn:
- *why relationships are so vital to your baby's psychological development*
- *how to relate to your baby in ways that encourage bonding*
- *night time parenting habits that strengthen your bond with baby.*

Your baby, the born socialite

There have been lots of theories about what might be the key factor that put our species on track to becoming such an intelligent sort of animal. Is it to do with tool use? To do with hunting in groups? To do with language?

Human babies are born exceptionally incapable of fending for themselves. As humans, it takes us up to two decades to get on top of the practicalities of daily life, and for our first half-decade we are very deeply dependent on older individuals for basic needs. This long period of immaturity gives us time to develop our big brains, and time to explore, speculate and learn about our world. But experts – especially the ones with children of their own – have long been puzzled by a question that will occur to you as a parent, pretty forcibly, sooner rather than later: how did nature 'expect' mothers, or even mothers and fathers together, to cope with the huge neediness of a baby? Most of us, after all, have a lot of help. Even if we have no nurse or cleaner, most of us do have access to washing machines, supermarkets, and all the rest. And yet, with a new baby in the house, there doesn't feel much time in the day for hunting and gathering, even at the supermarket. The investment of time and energy human children require is huge, way beyond that required by any other animal.

The latest research suggests that human mothers, or even human mothers and fathers together, never have been able to cope without help. We came to be human by finding ways of sharing the care of babies. This may be an important difference between human beings and other great apes, whose babies are cared for pretty exclusively by their mothers. You will not see a mother chimpanzee handing round her newborn for the admiration of friends and relations: she is fiercely possessive. But in almost all human societies, a newborn baby is handled and cooed over by a variety of friends and relations, and those friends and relations continue to play a role throughout childhood. The latest evidence suggests that our extended childhoods, with their unique possibilities for growth, learning and exploration, have always depended upon a network of aunts, uncles, friends, grandfathers and, especially, grandmothers, to help out with child-care. Hillary Clinton was not far off when she suggested that it 'takes a village' to raise a child. So **never feel you 'ought' to be able to care for your baby without help.** You will do the best job as a brain trainer if you accept appropriate offers of help.

Depending on the care of others not only buys human babies a longer time to learn. It also requires special kinds of intelligence from babies. Babies need to be able to recognize, seek out, win over, and then get along with suitable care-givers in their social group. Unlike baby chimpanzees, human babies seem to be evolved to be cared for by others as well as their mother. Letting responsible and loving friends and relations care for your baby some of the time is healthy as long as the baby is happy, and it will not weaken your bond with them.

The most basic way babies get the care they need is through crying. Many other baby animals cry for help, which makes the familiar idea that human babies cry to manipulate their parents particularly implausible. But the cry of a human baby does cause a very intense emotional reaction in nearby adults. The sound of your own baby's cry – and, to a lesser degree, of any baby – will trigger a powerful chemical surge in your own brain, prompting you to do all you can to help. Leaving your baby to cry will not only raise their stress levels, it will also raise yours.

Babies are also born with faces designed to melt your heart and win your care. Many baby mammals share the chubby, snubbed appearance of human babies, the recessive chin and forehead, blunt nose and big eyes. Adults are programmed to love and care for creatures that look like this.

One of the first skills your baby will master, is the charm offensive. Babies are way more endearing than Hugh Grant or Joanna Lumley. Their first moist, pearly-pink beams really do disarm and charm you and, very soon, they can turn them on to anyone within range. You have to be pretty hard-nosed to turn away from a baby whose grinning face and excited waving arms are inviting you to play. Notice, too, that baby is unwilling to turn away from you when you smile at them. They will usually give you at least a polite half-smile, as though anxious not to hurt your feelings.

We call those early dazzling smiles and heart-melting coos, 'engaging behaviours', because they are designed to do just that. The fact that, during the first nine months, babies are so free with their smiles, suggests that they are seeking to win over a wide circle of admirers.

Emotions and intelligence

You might expect a book about brain training to focus on cultivating your baby's intelligence. But what do we mean by that, exactly? Abstract intelligence, of the sort measured by IQ tests, isn't, in itself, the sort of thing many parents aspire to for their children. If the emotional functions of the brain are disrupted, even the most intelligent person won't be able to hold down a job or get pleasure from life. Practical intelligence is utterly dependent on emotional wellbeing. Stressed adults perform less well in IQ tests, and children also cannot fulfil their potential if they are tense. But more fundamentally, children are only willing and able to solve life's problems if they believe that they and their choices matter, if they feel capable of succeeding, and unafraid of failure, and if they feel comfortable with who they are. If you give your baby the love they need during their first few years, you will give them a gut feeling that the world is a loving place. This is life's most important gift; its legacy lasts a human a lifetime.

BONDING

Here is where the link between intelligence and emotion becomes really intricate. Science has established that babies need love to help their brains to grow. It's a fact that only confirms parents' deep intuition that every child needs love before anything else. But by loving your child, letting them know that they can trust you always to care for them, you also teach them lessons about human relationships that will be crucial for their own ability to form relationships in the future. Towards the end of the first year of life, and during the second, babies become markedly dependent on a few special people. They develop separation anxiety when they are parted from them, and begin to save their brightest smiles for these individuals alone.

Psychologists have long observed that assessing the quality of the bond between babies and their main care-givers is a way of predicting these children's emotional adjustment years, and even decades, down the line. This is because, just as your baby learns during the first years, from toys and other things, about the way physical objects behave, and from the conversations your baby hears, about how language works, so too they learn about people from their interaction with their nearest and dearest.

One piece of heart-rending research shows this vividly. One-year-old babies were shown animations of a big circle and small circle. At one point, the small circle begins to shake and cry. In one version of the animation, the larger circle rolls towards the small circle, to 'help', and in the other version it rolls away. The babies whose behaviour the psychologist had assessed as revealing a secure bond with their mothers looked much longer at the cartoon where the larger circle rolled away. They found it puzzling and surprising. But the babies who behaved as though their bond with their mothers was insecure, looked longer at the cartoon with the 'helpful' big circle. They found that behaviour surprising. By the time of their first birthday, babies have learned what to expect from the adults close to them.

Making sure your baby feels secure in their relation to you is not rocket science. Even a big circle, it seems, can show it cares!

We are born to be our babies' brain trainers, and babies are born to get the most out of us. During pregnancy, and even before, our own brains prepare us emotionally for the job. A lot of what we say in this book should confirm your instinctive approach to interacting with your baby. People close to babies naturally use lots of tricks to comfort them, to teach them language and other skills. Feel confident in your intuitions, and be very wary of parenting advice that makes you anxious, or that feels wrong. The advice to let babies cry it out is a good example. Parents who follow sleep-training programmes find them emotionally traumatic – we have seen mothers crying desperately outside the bedroom door – and it turns out that they are absolutely right to feel uneasy. If any of the suggestions in this book don't feel right to you when you try them, don't keep at them.

In some extreme cases, though, humans' instincts tell them not to care for their babies. In times of extreme famine, for example, our ancestors might have abandoned their babies, their instincts telling them they would not be able to keep both themselves and their child alive. The same instinctive mechanism might have led them to abandon very premature babies or sick children. We cannot entirely shake off our evolutionary past, so when you are depressed or extremely stressed, your bond with your child comes under strain. If the sound of your baby's cry does not motivate you to comfort them, and if the joy of their smile does not reach you, or if you ever feel the temptation to hurt your baby, these are signs that you need help. Your instincts are telling you that you need extra resources and support to raise your child.

ALWAYS RESPOND TO YOUR CHILD'S CRY, AS QUICKLY AS YOU CAN

Research has shown what anyone who knows anything about evolutionary theory knew already: the idea that responding to a baby's cry will in some way spoil them makes no sense. Babies who are attended to when they cry during infancy grow up to be toddlers and children who cry *less*. Your response to your baby's cry gives them their first experience of control and agency. They will learn to trust and rely on you, and this trust will be the foundation for all the other relationships of their life.

START 'CHATTING' WITH YOUR BABY FROM THE VERY START

It is easy to assume that all a very young baby needs is to be fed, clothed and helped to sleep. But they need conversation just as much, right from the word go. Babies are born with a marked preference for the sound of human voices, and the look of human faces, and they are able to conduct social exchange before they can do almost anything else. Eye contact is followed by smiles, then laughs, waving arms, whimsical expressions, coos, babbles, clapping, peeping, waving, showing and pointing, and then other signs and real words. During the first years, your baby will do most of their learning through the warm engagement of this kind of 'conversation'.

GIVE SMILES BACK

If your baby smiles or gazes at you, try to be alert to give smiles back – though of course your baby will not be traumatized if you happen to be craning your neck to see what their big sister is up to behind the sofa! Research shows that the babies of mothers who are depressed, and who therefore have difficulty returning smiles, have more depressed brain activity patterns and chemistry than the babies of contented mothers.

CUDDLE, SNUGGLE AND KISS AS MUCH AS YOU CAN

Loving physical contact continues to trigger cascades of bonding, brain-power nurturing chemicals in your baby's body as the months go by. Sometimes at the end of a long day, a loving hug or nuzzle is easier to get right than any other form of parental care. Babies are made to make us want to squeeze them, cycle their cubby legs and blow on their necks. Follow your instinct.

RESPOND TO AND RESPECT YOUR BABY'S LONGING TO BE PHYSICALLY CLOSE TO YOU

Don't listen to voices that tell you that baby ought to be happy sleeping on their own, sitting alone in their pram or highchair, or waiting alone for you while you pop out of the room to fetch something. You can gently encourage them to get used to various forms of physical separation, but there is nothing wrong with a baby who just wants to be held. In fact, your baby has healthy, evolved intuitions that they are safest, and will learn most, when they are close to you.

KEEP YOUR LANGUAGE POSITIVE

Research has revealed that parents differ greatly in the proportion of positive and negative exclamations they make to their babies. Some use several times more prohibition words – 'don't', 'stop', 'bad' – than others. Your baby will be happier and learn more quickly if you keep your language mainly positive. Using positive words will also keep your own attitude positive, and will strengthen your bond with baby.

Sleeping

The time when your baby's longing to be close to you is likely to raise the biggest parenting decisions is at bedtime. In our society many babies sleep alone in cots, and even in their own rooms. But babies are programmed strongly to protest at this kind of separation at sleep time, when they are at their most vulnerable. A baby human left to sleep alone in the environment in which we humans evolved would not have survived long. Some baby mammals, usually ones who live in safe burrows, instinctively keep quiet when their mother leaves them, so as not to attract predators. But human babies cry because they feel their lives depend upon summoning a caring adult.

Where, when, and how should baby sleep to optimize their brain development, and to maintain and strengthen the bond with their care-givers that is so crucial to that development? Considering how basic sleep is, we know surprisingly little about it. We know it is important – too little sleep and neither baby's body nor brain will grow properly. But apart from that, there is little consensus. As a tired parent, one of your greatest desires is probably for your baby to sleep long and deeply at night, and at nap time too. But as a brain trainer, what should your goals be? And how can you best achieve them?

Decisions about night regimes are complex. You need to weigh the evidence against the details of your own particular circumstances to find the best solution for your family.

Here are the facts you should know about this issue:

▶ Your baby is safer sleeping in the same room as you during the first six months. Lots of research confirms this, and it is common sense that your baby is safer if you can hear and see them, and get to them immediately if there is a problem.

▶ Having baby in bed with you is potentially dangerous *if* you do not observe safety precautions. This is another fact confirmed by research. Unfortunately, while most parents do sometimes sleep with their young babies, if they do so 'by accident' or without being prepared to do so, it can be a risky business for the baby.

▶ Sleeping on a sofa with baby is dangerous.

▶ Breastfeeding is more likely to be successful if baby sleeps in your bed. The sense of baby's body near yours will reinforce the hormonal balance that promotes your milk supply. Baby will be able to feed whenever they need to, without fully waking themselves or you.

▶ Baby's sleep patterns will be different if they sleep with you, and they will sleep less deeply.

▶ Most babies will strongly protest sleeping on their own. Some babies can get used to sleeping on their own – but almost all will be very upset about it to begin with.

▶ 'Sleep training' will produce huge changes in your baby's brain chemistry, and make them more stressed in the short term.

▶ Many societies consider it cruel to let a baby sleep alone.

▶ In many societies, including developed countries like Japan, it is quite usual for babies to share beds with adults.

▶ If baby sleeps in bed with you, you are likely to be woken more often each night, but to end up with significantly more sleep than if your baby sleeps in a cot.

▶ Some doctors believe a properly prepared cot to be the safest place for a newborn to sleep; others consider the parents' bed, properly prepared, to be safest.

There are a few other things scientists suspect about sleep regimes, but cannot be sure of, because the research has not yet been done:

▶ Letting baby sleep in your bed, having taken precautions, may be safer than having them sleep in a cot.

▶ The lighter sleep patterns characteristic of a baby sharing the parental bed may be better for its brain development.

- ▶ 'Sleep training' may alter your baby's brain in the long term, and make them less able to handle stress as an adult.
- ▶ Sharing a bed encourages interaction, bonding and security.

While there is not yet enough evidence for us to say for certain that co-sleeping is best for your baby's brain development, one message does come out clearly from recent research. **Sleep training that involves periods of crying is not good for your baby's brain.** When a baby left alone to sleep cries, they are not trying to control their parents, nor are they acting spoilt. Their instincts tell them that getting their parents back is crucial, a matter of life or death. Their brain is flooded with the stress hormone, cortisol. After a while your baby may stop crying, but this does not mean they have cheered up. In fact, the level of cortisol in their brain actually *rises* and they are more stressed than before. They have given up hope of help; they are reserving their strength and hiding from any hyenas on the prowl by keeping quiet. High cortisol levels may eventually lead their brain to shut itself off in sleep. So if your baby ceases to protest when you leave them at night, it can be a sign of greater stress than was the initial howling.

Apart from the distress sleep training causes your baby in the short term, recent research suggests high levels of cortisol may damage your baby's brain in the long term. Specialists believe repeated experiences of high stress in early life may render the adult brain less able to cope with stress. Advocates of controlled crying argue that only a minority of baby care writers believe it is harmful. True – that would be the minority who know about brain development! You will not find many brain scientists happy to support parenting gurus' confidence that sleep training is a healthy way of building independence and self-comforting strategies.

HOW TO SHARE YOUR BED WITH BABY IN SAFETY AND COMFORT

Whether or not to share a bed with your babies is a complex decision – though we can strongly recommend it from our own experience! If you do decide to do so, here are some tips:

Make sure baby lies on their back
Lots of research shows that baby is safer sleeping on their back than on their side. If your baby is in bed with you, you can make sure they stay on their back all night.

Check the mattress
Your mattress must not be too puffy or soft – get rid of soft mattress-toppers. A water-mattress, or any other sleeping surface that allows baby to roll in towards your body, is not safe. In Japan, where bed-sharing is the norm, firm futons are used.

Dump the duvet
Duvets are too puffy, thick, and inclined to shift around and smother a sleeping baby. Until your baby is at least seven months old, use cotton or fleece blankets instead.

...and the pillows
Soft pillows should be kept away from baby. If you are uncomfortable without one, use a small firm foam pillow instead of one stuffed with feathers or hollow-fibre, and keep most of the pillow behind you and away from baby.

Watch out for allergies
Help keep baby's breathing clear by washing your bedding frequently, and covering your mattress with a hypoallergenic mattress cover.

Baby should be next to mother only
While a baby is very young, its mother's sleep patterns and night-time awareness are radically altered so she is aware of her infant during sleep. This may not be true of the baby's father or for other siblings, so baby should not lie next to them.

Secure the edge of the bed
Check that the edge of the mattress near where baby sleeps is pushed firmly against a wall or other immovable vertical surface, so that there is no way baby can fall out of bed or get stuck down the side.

No soft toys or other puffy objects
Baby's place to sleep should be clear and empty.

Keep the room coolish
Around 17° Celsius (66° Fahrenheit) is ideal. Baby will be much warmer near you than they would be in a cot on their own. If you are comfortable, baby should be comfortable too – one of the advantages of having them so close.

Dress carefully, to match each other
It is safest if blankets are kept well below baby's armpits. This means you should resist the temptation to pull blankets up over your shoulders so that they cover baby too. Both you and baby should be dressed so that your upper bodies are warm enough without blankets. Baby needs to be only slightly more warmly dressed than you are, especially if their body will be against yours all night.

Sleep facing towards baby, with your head level with theirs
Always sleep with your face and body orientated towards baby. Ideally, for your baby to reap maximum benefit from being near you, your breath should tickle their skin, and you should keep in skin-to-skin contact. If you sleep on your side, curl your knees up below baby's feet, and let their foot and leg on the side nearest you touch your bare tummy. Your top hand or arm can go on their legs or hips, your other arm above their head. Keep your head level with your baby's – that way you will not be able to unconsciously pull the blanket over baby's head without also pulling it over your own.

Warning: Never let your baby share your bed if you are very overweight, smoke, have been taking drugs or drinking alcohol, or are exceptionally exhausted.

Childcare options

This is another big question for parents, and something every brain trainer will consider – who should take care of baby? In our society, most mothers are leaving their babies for extended periods each week before the end of the first year. The proportion of mothers who do so has soared in recent decades, and much research has been done to determine the effects of different forms of childcare on babies under two.

While findings have sometimes been conflicting, the great majority of serious studies have found that, all things being equal:

▶ babies from the most deprived social backgrounds may be given an edge in later IQ tests by attending high quality day care nurseries.
▶ for babies overall though, no such advantage is gained. Children in general score similarly in later IQ tests whether they attended day care or not.

- ▶ the higher the level of education of baby's main carers, the higher their IQ score will tend to be later on.
- ▶ while effects on IQ are subtle, babies who are in day care for the greatest number of hours each week are much more likely to experience mental health problems such as depression and attention deficit disorder later in childhood than are babies who are cared for at home.
- ▶ being cared for by a relative or nanny, rather than in a nursery, makes a child less likely to suffer mental health problems later on.
- ▶ the quality of a nursery is very important, especially the attitude and behaviour of carers and the ratio of carers to children.
- ▶ many children in day care experience elevated levels of the stress hormone cortisol, and continue to do so for weeks and months after they may seem to have 'settled in'.

It is quite clear that, *all things being equal*, your baby will be less vulnerable to mental health problems later on if they are mostly cared for either by their parents or by other loving adults, in the home, during their first two years. If your level of education is higher than that of the nursery nurses in the day care centre you would choose, being cared for by you instead is also likely to boost your baby's IQ.

On the other hand, *all things are not necessarily equal*. Recent research has shown that, if you take into account the downsides experienced by some stay-at-home mothers and their babies, there is little difference in outcomes for babies cared for at home as opposed to day care. Many parents feel lonely, isolated and overburdened at home alone with a young infant. This is quite normal: parents are biologically programmed to enjoy caring for their own babies in sociable and supported circumstances, but evolution has *not* prepared us for modern conditions in which one parent is often left to take care of a young infant all day long on their own.

If you find that being at home alone with your baby causes you real stress or depression, you should take your response seriously and feel reassured that it is perfectly natural.

Research shows that babies cared for by depressed mothers are at a big disadvantage in terms of emotional development, so it makes no sense to suffer in silence for the sake of your baby.

Many families also face financial difficulties if one stays off work to care for a baby, and again, if these difficulties lead to stress, depression or serious practical difficulties for parents, this is a bad result for their baby. While you should be in no doubt that having you all to themselves will make much more difference to your baby than whether or not you can afford lots of toys or a big house, having you to themselves will do him no good at all if you are constantly worrying about how to make ends meet.

You can try to look for a compromise. Many mothers enjoy working part-time, and the outcomes for babies are much better if they do not spend the whole of every day in day care. Again, time spent with a loving relative will also benefit your baby. If you decide to use a nursery or nanny, take the selection process seriously. For young children, the most important factor is the amount of warm, personal, one-on-one attention that is available.

If you do decide to care for your baby yourself full time, both of you will benefit from frequent outings and meetings with other mothers and babies. Make sure you find ways of being able to comfortably breastfeed in public places, so that feeding does not make it harder for you to get out and about. If you are able to care for your baby yourself full time for the first two years, and even beyond, your hard work and devotion will provide the ideal environment for the development of their brain.

If, on the other hand, full-time baby care is really impossible for you to manage, simply do your best to fill the time you do spend with your baby with emotional warmth, and don't waste time feeling bad about a decision that has been forced upon you. Many babies thrive in day care, especially if the hours they spend there are not too extended.

If your baby does not seem able to settle in to day care, on the other hand – if, after a couple of weeks, they still seem to dread being left there, seem less playful than before, or stop gaining weight, you need to come up with a new plan. A different nanny or nursery, or shorter hours, may suit your baby better. Take both your own and your baby's emotional needs seriously.

Bond-building brain games

All sorts of play builds the bond between yourself and your baby, but here are a few games that really play to your baby's sociable side.

PEEP-O

Here is a game that baby will love for a long time to come, and which can be elaborated as your baby grows:

▶ The first step is to catch your baby's eyes, with a look of excited expectation. Then hide behind the doorframe, or cover your face with something, and say 'Where's daddy/mummy?' When baby is very young, leave part of your face showing, so that they know you are still there. Then pop out with an excited 'Boo!', 'Hi!' or 'Here s/he is!' Your excitement and sound effects are key to the fun. You can also try gently covering baby's face with a hat or a hanky, saying, 'Where's baby? Oh there s/he is!'

▶ The next stage is, while close to baby, to cover your head or face with a cloth or hat, and then let them uncover you. This is one of the first games siblings can play together – the older one will love being uncovered by the scrabbling little hands of baby!

▶ Once baby is mobile, you can hide behind the couch (of course baby needs to see you do so), ready to great them with a delighted squeal and hug when they come round to find you.

Sometime late in the first year, baby may begin to initiate the game themselves by peeping from behind something or covering their own face with a hanky.

Peep-o is a great game because it involves a predicable sequence that builds baby's powers of anticipation, as well as their capacity for sociable turn-taking and face-to-face interplay. It may also help baby learn that when you are out of sight, you will always come back to them, and so make their attachment to your more secure.

MIRROR GAMES

As you carry baby around the house or the shops, stop at mirrors and wave hello. Baby will enjoy seeing you both together. Make your most animated faces, and say, 'It's baby!' You can pull silly faces in the mirror too, cuddling baby at the same time. After a while, baby may enjoy peeping at you in a mirror as a variation of peep-o.

CHARLIE CHAPLIN ROUTINES

You can begin building baby's sense of humour, a key to intelligent social interaction and bonding, from the very earliest days. Babies seem to have a natural love of slapstick comedy. Indulge it by pulling silly faces, flopping your hair over your eyes, jumping up and down like a frog, pretending to fall over, banging yourself on the head with a ball, juggling and then dropping something, pretending to sneeze – nothing is too silly. Keep eye contact and an animated expression, and include lots of silly sound effects like 'booof!' and 'boioioing!' and baby will be your most appreciative audience ever. Notice how the same tricks may not raise even a small smile in your baby if you do them with a straight face: already they have learned to share a mood and to follow social cues.

ROLL A BALL

Sit face-to-face with your baby and roll or toss a ball to and fro between you. At first you will need to collect it from your baby's lap, but by the end of the first year they may start to return it. Chat as you play – 'Throw the ball to Ruby – here you go! – and back to Mummy – there we go!' This is another face-to-face game that builds anticipation, turn-taking and social bonding.

HOW BIG IS BABY?

Say to your baby, 'How big are you, baby?' or, even better, use their own name. Answer your own question, 'This big!' Show your baby how to raise their arms up as high as they can when you say 'This big'. Eventually they will get the hang of the game and raise their arms themselves.

ROUND AND ROUND THE GARDEN

This is one of those traditional games that combines anticipation, language and loving touch, showing that parents through the ages have had a great intuitive sense of how best to train their babies' brains. In case you don't know the game, it goes like this: trace your finger round and round on your baby's palm, tummy or back, and say 'Round and round the garden, like a teddy bear' – then walk your fingers up to your baby's armpit or neck – 'One step, two step … tick-l-y under there!' and tickle under your baby's chin.

THIS LITTLE PIGGY

Another traditional game which turns bonding into learning. Start with baby's big toe and work along the toes, tweaking each one. 'This little piggy went to market, this little piggy stayed home, this little piggy had nice roast beef, but this little piggy had none, and this little piggy went wee wee wee all the way home' – walk your fingers up to a tickly place and tickle.

BODY PARTS

Help your baby learn where their body parts are by playing games. Ask, 'Where's your nose?' Then show them where their nose is. Then ask, 'Where's Mummy's nose?', and show them that. Then rub noses, saying, 'Nose, nose, nose!' Try something similar with as many different bits of baby as they seem to enjoy, naming and squeezing as you go along.

ANIMAL SOUNDS

Help baby learn animal sounds. For example, ask, 'What does the cow say?' and make a hilarious moo in reply. Actions are fun too. Flap baby's arms for 'bird', butt them with finger-horns for 'cow', and hop them up and down for 'frog', and so on. Your baby will eventually make some of the animal actions and noises of their own accord.

YOUR TURN

▶ Take your baby's emotional needs seriously. It is natural that they want to be close to you. Always respond to their cries and appeals for closeness.

▶ Take your own emotional reactions seriously too. Don't follow advice that seems harsh, or try to parent in a particular way just because everyone else does it like that.

▶ If you feel you cannot respond to your baby with the consistent warmth that they need to form a strong bond with you, seek some help.

▶ Encourage your baby to form warm, trusting bonds with a range of other people.

▶ Take the time to establish a sleep routine that suits the family but that will not stress your baby.

▶ Avoid sleep-training regimes that involve crying.

▶ Think carefully about who should look after your baby during the day. Make a decision that suits the particular needs of you and your baby.

▶ If you are hiring a nanny, be very careful about who you choose, putting emotional warmth and engagement at the top of your list of requirements.

▶ If you enjoy looking after your baby all day, be confident that they will benefit from this and that it is worth making other big changes to make it possible.

▶ If your baby seems less happy after beginning day care, find them another care situation that suits them better.

▶ Play face-to-face bonding games with your baby as often as you can.

4

....

Physical skills and brain power

In this chapter you will learn:
- *how baby's physical progress is related to their intelligence*
- *what you can do to help baby reach the next physical milestone*
- *how to create an environment that helps baby learn new physical skills.*

Physical development and intelligence: is there a link?

We might be inclined to think that if there is a relation between baby's physical and mental skill, it is an inverse relation. At school and later on, many individuals focus either on physical or academic achievement, and don't excel at both.

But babies don't work that way. Some of the first things a baby learns are about the basics of physical things, including their own limbs, and how they move about and interact in space. During the first year, there is huge growth in the areas of the brain – the parietal lobe and the motor cortex – that process spatial relations, touch, and controlled body movement. For the first several years of life, some of the most important things, and the most important ways that a child learns, involve active interaction with the world. To affect their environment, and so learn about agency, cause and effect, and problem-solving, a baby needs to be able to control their own body. For babies, getting physical is not just 'sport', but the first vital step towards understanding the world and their place in it.

Of course, some babies *are* quicker to reach mental milestones than they are to reach physical ones, or the other way round. But building your baby's muscles will not divert energy from building their brain.

There may be truth in the idea that baby is not learning any new baby signs at the moment because they are busy working on their first independent steps – babies do seem to focus on one particular task a week – but taking those first steps involves brain work and provides new stimulation and information for the brain to work on.

HOW YOUR BABY'S PHYSICAL SKILLS AFFECT THEIR MENTAL DEVELOPMENT

If you think about a physical skill like sitting up, it's clear how physical development might help babies learn new mental skills. Once babies can sit up alone, they have far more control over what they look at. They can turn around to look for you, wherever you go, or turn away when they get bored. In fact, what they do is suddenly far more a matter of their own choice. They can reach out and choose between different toys, putting them down and picking them up.

With crawling, even more new possibilities open up. Around the time babies are learning to think about objects that are out of sight, some of them can crawl round the corner to check what has happened to them. Research confirms that babies who are mobile seem to understand object permanence (the idea that an out of sight object still exists), much better than non-mobile babies. Of course, a mobile baby can also crawl off to find the action if they get bored, which must help the learning process.

In adults, exercise produces endorphins that make us feel good, and promote relaxation. There's no reason to think this is different for babies, and a happy and relaxed baby can learn faster.

HOW MUCH DIFFERENCE CAN YOU MAKE TO YOUR BABY'S PHYSICAL DEVELOPMENT?

We take it for granted that training makes a huge difference when it comes to marathon running or gymnastics, but can training change the speed at which babies acquire physical skills, too? It seems that it can. Research recording the age at which babies develop particular capacities across different cultures suggests that different cultural practices have quite marked effects on the age at which babies do things like sit up and walk. In many traditional societies, mothers put infants through a complex regime of stretching and exercise to help them reach their milestones. In some places, they dig little pits in the ground to support their babies in an upright position until they can sit up alone. These babies sit alone more than a month earlier, on average, than American babies. On the other hand, the babies of some South American rainforest tribes are brought up in an environment where it is too dangerous to put them down on the ground. They are carried constantly for the first few years of life, and walk months or even years later than the average American baby.

Mind you, if your goal is to produce an Olympic athlete, physical baby training won't help much. Early differences in achieving physical milestones between cultures do *not* seem to correlate with later physical ability. Big differences in the first year soon disappear. Those rainforest toddlers who couldn't walk become the most amazing gymnasts within months of taking their first steps!

But physical baby training is an indirect form of brain training, because it helps get your baby into a better position for learning.

FIVE WAYS YOU CAN HELP YOUR BABY OVERCOME THEIR PHYSICAL LIMITS

1 Dress baby for action
While there is no need to invest in a three to six month lycra leotard with speed stripes, do think about the way you dress your baby. Societies where babies are very wrapped up tend to have babies who reach physical milestones later. When you are as small and weak as a newborn, clothing can really make movement difficult. In a modern, centrally-heated home, baby does not need to be dressed in several layers. When they are awake, they need no more clothes than you do, and if they are in your warm arms, they may need fewer. Be especially wary of thick padded jackets and snowsuits. These hamper movement and may even get between baby's hands and mouth, which is a real annoyance. Padded suits are only necessary for cold winter days when baby is in a pram and not next to your body. Snug-fitting warm hats are a better way of keeping your baby warm outside, as they don't get in the way, and most of the heat is lost through the top of your baby's big head. Watch out for goose pimples as a sign that they need more clothes.

Don't let baby spend too long in scratch mittens. Bringing their hands to their face and mouth is one of the first skills your baby will develop, and mittens will spoil the fun. If your baby is a real nose-scratcher, mittens during the night are okay, but it's best to try to keep their nails short, and not worry too much about the odd scrape they give themselves during the day.

Make sure babygros and sleep-suits fit well. If they are too small, your baby will not be able to extend their legs fully, which is another early skill they will be working on. If they are too big, arms and legs will get lost in the fabric.

Try to keep nappies as well-fitted as possible, to avoid binding waistlines and bulky crotches.

2 Make changing-time a workout
Tying baby exercises to the nappy-changing routine will help make sure baby gets enough training to make a difference.

Except when there have been sudden explosions, try to change your baby when they are content and active. Make sure your changing stations are comfortable and safe. A mat on the floor might be more comfortable for you and safer for your baby than a table, especially as your baby gets bigger. Have kitchen paper and a towel at hand to catch unexpected fountains that happen during nappy-off time. Some babies can't stand the cold feel of a plastic changing mat. You might need a towel or piece of fleece laid over it to make it more comfortable. Try to change baby in a room that is warm enough for them to be comfortably naked in for a while.

Baby will soon take the removal of their nappy as a signal that it's playtime. Soon after birth, and for a few months, they will love kicking and flapping their arms, often making adorable noises as they do so. When they stop, gently cycle your baby's legs, or jiggle them up and down, giving their bottom a little bounce. Roll them from side to side, and onto their tummy. Nuzzle your baby's chest and let them pull your hair. Move gently and slowly, but get used to the feel of your baby, all the things they can do and the things they can't quite do yet.

3 Become a climbing frame
You may not be used to thinking of yourself as a cutting edge, multi-functioning piece of gym equipment, but that's one of the ways your baby sees you. You may notice that they can sit up, pull themselves to standing, and combat-crawl forward on you, several weeks before they can do those things on the floor. Your body is endlessly adaptable to your baby's rapidly changing size and strength, and has few hard edges for them to fall against. The terrain is great for the wiggling which is a baby's first form of locomotion. Even newborns

seem to be able to make progress towards the milk supply across their mother's stomach.

From the very first days, babies enjoy being dandled in a lap or being jiggled on your sloped knees as you gently bounce them by pulling their arms towards you. Soon things get even more exciting. Baby will stand with their tummy against your sloping shins, arm folded over the top, pull themselves up on your clothes to reach your nose, or go off-roading over your body and plunge over its edge into the pillows. By this stage, bed is the safest place for the wilder workouts. But the workouts shouldn't be limited to a couple of times a day. Whenever your baby is awake and in your lap, encourage them to stand or jump holding your fingers, bounce in your lap looking over your shoulder, climb down your back as you hold on at the knees, or pursue whatever other mad caper takes their fancy.

When they are playing on the floor, lie nearby and let them climb over you. Put your hands or legs behind their feet when they are on their stomach, so they can push off against you and move forward. Stretch out an arm for them to pull up on. Lift them high above your body to kick and practise their balance.

4 Choose the right resting places

In many developed countries, it is traditional to put young babies down flat on their backs to rest and sleep, or simply to be out of the way while we get on with things. However, this isn't a universal or 'natural' state of affairs. In many cultures, babies usually take their daytime sleep on adult bodies, either in a lap or over a shoulder or moving around in a sling. And they rest in laps too, if not in that of their mother, then in that of a friend or relation.

Newborns, in particular, spend so much time just waking up or dozing off during the day, that the place they do it can make a big difference to their development. Babies can only exercise a narrow range of muscles and motor skills lying on their backs. And they can't see much. On the other hand, as we've noticed, babies can sit up in a lap from pretty early on, and they can peep over a shoulder from the word go.

We now know that it is not safe for young babies to sleep on their stomachs, and it is now uncommon for parents to let them do so. This has saved lives, but has a downside in that babies do not get as much practice lifting their heads and so tend to sit and crawl later.

Don't leave your baby flat on their back when they are awake. If there is a lap or shoulder available, let baby rest there, in a position that gives them a good view. If there isn't a spare lap, the bouncy baby seats with the metal frames are a good alternative. They give even a newborn baby a good view of what's going on. When baby is awake, a baby bouncer (once baby can hold their head steady) hung from a doorframe, or an inflatable baby nest, are also both good alternatives for moments when you need to put your baby down.

Once baby can sit up, make sure there is always a safe place for them to do so, well padded with thick rugs and cushions, so that you aren't tempted to lie them down instead.

5 ... and the right forms of transport

Children playing with dolls often rock them and carry them lying flat in arms like a cradle. That's how new parents often imagine themselves holding their baby. But this may not be the best way to carry a real baby. It's not particularly safe or particularly comfy for you, and it doesn't allow the baby to practise movement. Baby will get enough time in this position when they are being fed. So try instead to carry your newborn against your shoulder, with their head peeping over. At first they will rest their heavy head against your shoulder and neck, but they will have a good view. And very soon you will notice them turning, and then lifting their head. Even if you never hold them like this for more than five minutes, if you always carry them like this instead of in a cradle-hold, all those minutes put together will make a difference to their development. Some babies prefer to be carried facing forward. One hold that works is to hold them upright with their back against your chest and tummy, supporting their crotch with your hand, with your arm coming in front and across their body.

You also need to think about how you transport baby out and about. There are a very wide range of pushchairs and baby carriers to choose from. The best forms of transport should give your baby a good view and free movement when awake, but also provide a safe place to sleep. If a newborn's head slumps while they sleep, bending their neck forward and their chin onto their chest, it can restrict their breathing and the oxygen levels in their blood, which might be bad for their brain and other functions. For this reason, car seats that fit into travel systems, buggies that don't lie flat, and slings that hold baby in a curled up horizontal cradle-hold, may not be ideal places for a very young baby to sleep. This becomes less of an issue once your baby has good neck control.

A pushchair that reclines to flat but also allows baby to sit up progressively straight as they develop, allowing them to see and move when they are awake, will be a better investment than a traditional pram. Alternatively, there are many baby carriers that are very safe places for a newborn to sleep, and also very good for their physical development as they grow. The best of these keep baby upright, their neck straight and well-supported when they sleep, but free to move once they have the strength.

Rock your baby

The cerebellum is a part of the brain that plays an important role in movement and balance, and also in mental processes linked with language, social interaction, musical ability, attention, and probably in emotional reactions such as fear and enjoyment. Movements such as rocking, twirling and hanging upside-down encourage the development and growth of this part of the brain. Indeed, when baby was small enough to turn somersaults in the womb, they were probably working on their cerebellum. Now you need to make sure it gets enough stimulation in the outside world too. If you carry baby around a lot, this will help, as your movement includes up, down, sideways and rolling motions that fully activate your baby's inner ear. If rocking comforts baby, that will also work. If they enjoy a swing ride, indulge them, as it may also help build their brain. Once they are old enough, encourage them to enjoy spinning playground equipment, as well as just turning around until they feel dizzy – just be there to make sure they don't fall over!

TRAIN YOUR BABY TO SIT UP, IN FIVE STEPS

Baby's muscles develop control, tone and strength from the head down, as myelin builds up on the nerves that control their spine. Only when that development has reached the waist will they be able to sit alone. This is an exciting milestone, making life much easier for both babies and parents. Baby can now sit anywhere, as long as the floor around them is well padded. Their hands are free to play. Many baby books cite seven or eight months as the time you can expect baby to sit alone, but with encouragement some babies can do it before they reach four months. A few will wait till the second half of the first year despite all your efforts. This is nothing to worry about, just part of the infinite variety of babies. Your encouragement will bring that sitting moment forward.

1 You can start the sitting training during baby's first week. Regularly lie your baby on their stomach, and watch them make an effort to lift and turn their head. At first they may not be able to move it at all, but they will make fast progress, and in doing so will strengthen their neck and upper back muscles. It's good to start doing this very early, as an older baby may object to the 'beached' feeling of being on their stomach if they aren't used to it.

2 The next step can start when baby is a couple of weeks old. Each time you change their nappy, or whenever they are calm and interested, very gently pull your baby up by their arms to a sitting position. At first you should hold both their hands in one of your hands, and support their heavy head in the other. When they have a little more head control, so that, as you pull on their arms, you can see that they can support their head almost straight with their body as you lift, you can hold one of their hands in each of your own. Go very gently and slowly. Soon your baby will be able to hold their own head straight with their body, and then to tuck in their chin. One exciting day, you will see baby tuck in their chin in anticipation as you reach for their hands. Many babies visibly enjoy these exercises: they become like a dance you can do together.

3 Once baby can usually hold their head steady when you've pulled them up, see what happens if you let them lean forward. Keeping your hands just a whisker away from their shoulders, ready to catch, almost let go. At first, baby will flop forward from the waist, and the weight of their head will start to raise their bottom off the floor as they go into a full flop (control the flopping with your hands so that your baby doesn't hurt themselves!). Gradually, though, this will happen more and more slowly, so baby is bent double with their nose on the carpet for

a few moments before toppling forward. Soon, baby will start to use their hands to hold themselves up, putting off the topple even longer. At this stage, if you straighten them out into a sit, they will be able to look up at you for a moment or two before swaying off to one side or the other. Before long, the will be able to sit leaning propped forward on their hands. Lift your baby back upright, and watch them raise their arms for balance. They will be able to maintain that independent, upright sit for longer and longer each time.

4 Once baby can hold their head up and back straight, and just seems to need to learn to balance, invest in a baby seat that supports them in an upright sitting position. These are usually marketed for babies between three and nine months old, and may be too big for your three-month-old. If it is, you could tuck a towel around baby's back and sides (but not under their bottom, as that might make it possible for them to fall out of the seat). Alternatively, or as well, you can try other ways of propping up your almost-sitting baby. If it is summer and you have a sandpit or spend time at the beach, you may be able to dig a baby-bottom shaped hole in the sand and line it and the surrounding sand with a towel. In the house, rolled up sheets curled into a horseshoe shape can work well. You may find it helps to tuck up baby's feet a bit as well. Baby can now practise sitting, even while your hands are not around to catch them.

5 Once baby can sit upright for a short time, encourage them to do so by dangling toys just above their eye level, to encourage them to look up. Stretch your baby's ability by moving the toys to one side, so that they need to twist to see them. See if they can reach forward for a toy on the floor and then sit up again. Keep moving the toy's location, to see how far forward they can reach and still get up again. Even after sitting is looking very steady, it will be months before you can trust your baby not to fall over. At first, the falls will be mostly backwards, and the whack this could inflict on the back of your baby's head will not be fun, and could even make them fearful of sitting. Later, falls will be mainly forward, as baby reaches for a far-off toy and loses balance. With these types of falls, their head can hit the floor a surprisingly long way from where their bottom is planted. So make sure your baby is in the middle of a good thick rug, with cushions behind and to the sides, or inside a play-nest or ring, which will break their fall.

DON'T FRET ABOUT CRAWLING

Sitting and walking are essential milestones that all normally developing babies must reach sooner or later. Crawling is not. Many babies never learn to crawl 'properly', but instead wiggle along on their stomachs, shuffle on their bottoms, or roll over and over to get where they want to be. Crawling is the most efficient way for a baby to move around before they have the balance to walk, and if you can help your baby get the hang of it, it may make life more fun for them during the second half of their first year. But if your baby is meeting other developmental milestones, there is no need to worry that they aren't crawling.

Insight: baby knows best!

At eight months, Tass showed no interest in crawling, insisting instead on walking holding someone's hand. We wondered whether we should 'make' him crawl by refusing our hands. But by nine months he walked alone, never having crawled. He reminded us that each baby develops in their own unique way.

Designing an environment for exploring

Playpens are fine for the brief moments when you just have to put your mobile baby down and leave the room, but a long stretch in a playpen is a baby's nightmare. It is just too predictable and restrictive for good learning, even if it's full of toys. Playpens also feed what may be a dangerous myth about babies – the idea that it's fine to leave them to themselves. In practice, it's very hard to leave a baby for more than a few seconds without putting them at risk of either boredom or injury. There is no substitute, in terms of safety and stimulation, for adult attention. Your baby needs at least half an eye on them all day long.

Even if you do watch baby carefully, they can still bang their head, pull down a lamp on themselves, or grab a knife or hot drink in the split second it takes before you can intervene. When your baby starts to crawl, do some baby-proofing. Try crawling around every part of every room in the house, looking for dangers at a baby's level. It will be very hard for you to make your house completely safe for baby to roam unsupervised without also making it very boring, but you need to remove those split-second hazards that even vigilance can't guarantee against. Most dangerous perils are plugs and sockets, hanging cables, tip-able furniture, and sudden drops on stairs and landings. It's really worth padding the sharp edges of coffee tables and the like, as baby's head will almost inevitably bang against them at some point as they explore. Glass ornaments should be out of reach, and so too should small, round, hard choking hazards.

Not a single baby reaches its second birthday without playing with many objects that would not pass safety tests if they were toys. Even books are potentially dangerous, as once ripped or broken they can become choking hazards, and they may contain dyes that baby should not be sucking on. As for the garden, it's full of potential hazards. This doesn't mean, though, that you should keep your baby inside and away from everything but toys designed for under threes. Doing that could compromise their development. They need a constant flow of new objects and spaces to explore. Try and give them closely supervised access to as many objects and parts of the house as you can. Many ordinary things are safe if you are close enough to stop the mucky gravel on its way to their lips, or to catch hold of the china vase before they can find out what happens if it's banged on the tile floor!

TRAIN YOUR BABY TO WALK, IN SEVEN STEPS

1 Many babies can support a lot of their own weight on their legs almost from birth. Instead of having baby lie or sit in your lap, 'dandle' them, that is, hold their hands and let them stand, leaning against your body if needs be. Your baby will take more and more of their own weight, until they are holding on only for balance. They may also like to bounce in your lap, which is great for their leg muscles. Encourage them by accentuating each bounce with a bit of a lift.

2 Support your baby's early efforts to pull up on furniture. If you notice them pull down on something that could bear their weight, support their bottom and help them lift themselves to their feet. They may be able to hold on once they are up there for a surprisingly long time. Babies vary hugely in the age at which they start to do this, but you should be watchful for signs of keenness from three or four months on.

3 Take a look at your furniture, and see if you can use it to encourage baby to pull up, stand and play. Look out for useful, solid drawer-handles good for pulling up on, or safely wedge

open drawers at baby's height. Remove tip-able furniture. Invest in cheap or second hand coffee and occasional tables – nested sets of three are common in charity shops. Stick self-adhesive Velcro pads to these and attach interactive toys, fitted with their own pads of Velcro. Plastic play tables are also great for keeping your baby on their feet. Remember, though, that your baby will still be very inclined to fall and bang themselves not only on the floor but also sidelong on whatever they are holding on to, so you need to be within catching distance.

4 Soon baby may try to reach a toy on the other side of their play table by edging around it, or 'cruising'. First they may move their feet across one another and get tangled; next they will move sideways, and after that they may turn their feet in the direction they want to go. Arrange a cruising circuit that might take in the sofa, small tables, open drawers, and even long curtains if they are securely hung. Baby may be motivated to practise their cruising if they can travel a really long distance.

5 Let your baby practise their walking out and about by letting them walk between your legs as you hold both their hands, between two adults as you hold a hand each, and then, when they have the balance, hold just one of their hands. Try to support less and less of their weight, by lowering the level of your hand, or letting them hold fewer and fewer of your fingers, until they are using you for balance alone. Some babies love to kick a ball in front of them when they practise walking like this.

6 You will know when your baby is nearly set for their first independent steps. The little hand holding yours as the two of you walk along will have a relaxed arm and a bent elbow. They will let go of their play table and stand independently for half a minute, while they examine a toy with both hands. Encourage early unsupported steps by leaving ever wider gaps in their cruising circuit, so that they need to be brave and take a step alone to get where they want to go. When they are standing alone, kneel close by and encourage them to come to your outstretched hands. If they have trouble turning their feet, they may find it easier to walk from a balanced independent stand between one grown-up's legs towards the outstretched hands of another. If baby tends to 'plummet' from one person to another, losing balance in their eagerness to get to their destination, try giving them a small soft toy or other distraction, and they may

saunter across the gap without even noticing what they are doing until they get there.

7 Once your baby can walk several steps independently, you can encourage their independence while keeping them safe by using a harness, with its long reins slack most of the time, but ready to catch them if they fall. Take them outdoors to places without traffic and with good even surfaces, where they can practise. At home on the carpet where falls won't hurt too much, see if they can squat or bend to pick up a toy and get up again and carry on.

Baby walkers won't help your baby walk

The sort of wheeled baby walker into the middle of which baby is inserted with their legs dangling down is unlikely to help with their walking. Research shows that, probably because they cannot see their feet and so lack an important bit of feedback, babies who use such walkers are actually slower, on average, to learn to walk. Some research even suggests they may be behind on other developmental fronts too. These walkers are also strongly linked with accidents, some of them serious. The walkers designed to be pushed along from behind by baby have had no such bad press, though the babies in our family find them too tippy to help much.

YOUR TURN

▶ Encourage your baby to be physically active right from birth. Don't think of them as a helpless bundle that should be wrapped up and laid down.

▶ Make sure you don't dress your baby in a way that restricts movement.

▶ Choose a pushchair or baby sling that encourages motor development.

▶ Avoid having your baby lie down flat when they are not asleep.

▶ Let your baby use your body as a climbing frame.

▶ Make sure you have safe spaces in every room for your baby to sit, crawl, and walk.

▶ Encourage your baby to hold up their head, to sit up, and then to walk around, by testing their physical abilities, and by using your own body to help them take each new step.

5

Food for brains

In this chapter you will learn:
- *about the brain benefits of breast feeding*
- *how to help your baby train their brain at mealtimes*
- *about the key nutrients your baby needs for brain building*
- *how to avoid foods that threaten brain development.*

Without a good enough diet, your child's brain will not be able to develop to its full potential. Everyone agrees about that. Some specialists also believe that a really good diet – as opposed to a diet that is just not too bad – can lead to enhanced brain development. Many experts have concerns about certain foodstuffs common in the modern diet, and the effect they may have on the brain in particular, as well as on general health. Healthy eating is important not only for the development of the brain, but also to maintain its chemistry day in, day out. Your baby will concentrate and learn better, and feel happier, if their brain is fed with a steady supply of nutrients.

It is becoming clear that diet in childhood, especially in the earliest years, has a profound effect on shaping adult eating habits. For instance, adult obesity can be predicted from a baby's weight at twelve months – and sometimes even as early as four months. On the other hand, the healthy eating habits they develop as a baby can stay with them throughout their life, helping them learn every day.

During the first year or two of life, you need to think not only about what baby eats, but *how* they eat it. Remember, it's the daily habits that make the big impact on your baby's brain development. If your baby spends an hour or more a day eating – and some babies spend much more than that – then how that eating happens will make a big difference to their daily experience.

Wonder milk

You will probably spend a couple of decades worrying to some degree about your child's diet. Bearing this in mind, you should enjoy the freedom from this worry that breastfeeding brings you in your baby's first year, if you possibly can. Breast milk is a food so perfect for babies that we are still isolating new, super-complex beneficial ingredients in it, month by month. A lot of research comparing breastfed and bottle-fed babies has linked breastfeeding with higher IQ – though the studies are hard to do because breastfeeding is a smart choice, which sifts out mothers with brainy genes.

Breast milk contains the perfect balance of fatty acids, which are crucial for myelination and brain development in general. The huge growth in the weight of your baby's brain during the first few years will be mainly made up of fats. Some researchers believe that breast milk can improve your child's memory for life, because it is an excellent source of choline, from which a baby's body makes the neurotransmitter acetycholine, essential for memory. Another brain-builder present in breast milk is taurine, which the body cannot make from other amino acids.

Breast milk also contains active infection-fighting antibodies, which make your child far less likely to suffer secondary infections in their ears or throat when they get a cold. Such infections can impair their hearing and interfere with learning as a result. Breast milk also offers some protection against more serious infections, such as meningitis, that can seriously harm the brain. In fact, it has far too many health benefits to list here!

Breastfeeding is also a perfect way of bonding with your baby, and bathing their brain and yours, in lovely, relaxing, happy-making neurotransmitters. In the vast majority of human societies throughout history, all women, except perhaps a few of the most wealthy, nursed their own babies. But our society is shamefully unfriendly to breastfeeding. Many mothers do not get the support they need learning how to breastfeed, and are made to feel embarrassed breastfeeding in public places by our society's bizarre hang-ups. The first week or two of breastfeeding can be difficult – even very difficult – and if you find it so please do get help. Some resources are listed at the back of the book.

Once you've got the hang of it, don't feel you should keep your feeding 'in the closet'. Breastfeeding is not just better for your baby; it is also far more convenient for you – as long as you can feed your baby whenever, and wherever, as nature intended. Remember that by feeding your baby in public, you are doing a service to babies everywhere by challenging absurd social taboos that make life worse for them and for their mothers.

If you breastfeed, you should let your baby decide exactly when and for how long they would like to feed. During the early weeks, you should offer them milk as often as you can. Soon, they will begin to let you know when they would like to suckle. They may want to suckle because they are hungry or thirsty, or they may want to suckle because their brain needs some of the feel-good chemicals that will be produced by the nursing process. In other words, they may want to suckle for comfort. These are two equally good reasons for your baby to nurse. As they begin to let you know they would like to nurse, and you begin to respond to their needs, your baby reaps extra rewards. They now have some control over an important part of their environment – not only their food supply, but also you. You are beginning to communicate, to build trust, and to understand each other.

There are many parenting books out there that suggest that your baby should not feed too often, and will be 'happier' if fed according to a three or four hour schedule. You may hear scientific-sounding justifications to do with fore- and hind-milk. There is no real science behind this advice, and following it may disrupt the earliest 'conversations' and structures of trust between you and your baby. (See *Further resources* for scientifically supported breastfeeding advice if you have problems.) Hear this: taking breastfed babies all over the world into account, the average gap between breastfeeding sessions is neither four nor three hours, but eighteen minutes.

If you cannot breastfeed your baby, don't waste time feeling bad about it. Artificial baby milk is getting better all the time, and you can give your baby some of the psychological benefits of breast feeding by holding them close against your skin and stroking their limbs while you feed them.

Super foods

Most research suggests that six months is the best age to begin to introduce your baby to solid food – though if your baby seems interested, you can introduce some of the nutrient-dense foods we discuss here anytime after four months. Some people call the process weaning, but remember that, if you are breastfeeding, the goal is not to wean your baby from the breast or to even to reduce the amount of milk your baby drinks. Breast milk continues to provide your baby with invaluable fatty acids and antibodies throughout the first year, and for as long as you and your baby are happy with your nursing relationship.

Perhaps the biggest reason to introduce solid food at this age is not nutritional at all but rather developmental. Around this age, baby will already have been obsessively mouthing everything in sight for some time. The potential for learning and having fun with food is huge. Your baby has a whole world of tastes and textures to explore, and will finally be able to practise their fine motor skills on small objects without your snatching them away in case your baby swallows them and chokes. Managing food in their mouth will also build the muscles they need for speech.

Another reason to introduce solid food, slowly, from this age onward, is that it may make your baby less likely to develop food allergies, which may have subtle effects on behaviour and brain function. Modern science knows relatively little about allergies. We do know, though, that in the case of wheat, babies who are fed the grain before four months are very much more likely to develop coeliac disease (a serious allergic response to gluten) later in life. On the other hand, babies who are not fed any wheat at all until after seven months are also rather more likely to develop coeliac disease. For this reason, wheat should be one of the first things on baby's menu at six months.

The main nutritional reason to introduce solid foods is that, in theory, a baby may not get enough iron from breast milk alone to last them into early childhood. Our understanding of the way the body uses iron is also incomplete, but most authorities recommend that babies' iron status is best protected by offering a mixed diet that includes iron-rich foods from six months onwards.

BABY-LED WEANING

You may have heard about baby-led weaning (BLW). If you follow this method, instead of pureeing food and spoon-feeding your baby, you allow baby to feed themselves. This is a fantastic learning opportunity for your baby, and also allows them another bit of control over an important part of their life. A baby breastfed on demand decides when and how much to eat. BLW allows your baby the same freedom when it comes to solids. All babies should get to feed themselves at least some of the time as soon as they are able to do so, for the sake of their brain development, the development of their fine motor skills, and to train the muscles in mouth and throat.

What about choking?

Experts think that babies who feed themselves may be less likely to choke than babies who are spoon-fed. By the time they are developed enough to get the food to their mouths and onto their tongues, babies are also well able to move the food around in there and spit out any lumps too big for them to handle. Babies who feed from a spoon, on the other hand, learn to suck food straight to the back of their mouths and down their throats, without control. Whether your baby is spoon- or self-fed, you should keep round, hard foods, like hard frozen berries, whole grapes, nuts, processed sausage, and large hard pieces of dried fruit away from them. Until they are a practised chewer, try also to avoid foods off which they could bite a hard piece, such as uncooked carrot sticks or long pieces of raw apple. Nevertheless, a self-fed baby is less likely to choke on a dangerous piece of food or toy than a spoon-fed one.

Gagging is not choking

While your self-feeding baby is very unlikely to choke on their food, they are very likely to gag on it. When your baby is choking, there is something stuck in their windpipe and they cannot cough or make much sound. When your baby is gagging, a piece of food is tickling the back of their mouth or the top of their throat, and they will cough and splutter, and maybe bring up a bit of their meal. Gagging is not 'almost choking', but rather one of the body's defences against choking. Baby can gag on things that they could not choke on, small bits that stick to the roof of their mouth and throat, such as fine bits of fruit skin and bits of salad leaf. Spoon-fed babies usually gag when they are introduced to lumpy food, but self-fed babies learn to gag effectively earlier on.

Top foods for BLW

If your baby is feeding themselves, they can have almost anything that the grown-ups are eating. If you eat a varied and healthy diet yourself, you won't have to think too much about designing your baby's menu. But some foods are particularly helpful in terms of the developmental side of eating, and others are worth eating more regularly because of their high nutritional value. Here are our top ten (not in any particular order):

1 Broccoli florets – easy to hold and full of vitamins and minerals. Steam or microwave until tender.
2 Ripe avocado wedges – a great texture for a beginner eater, and a good balance of nutrients, including lots of good fats.
3 Fine-cut organic liver strips – the best food for baby's iron levels and also the easiest meat for them to bite. Cut into fine slices before lightly frying in olive oil.
4 Well-cooked sweet potato and carrot wedges – full of great vitamins and easy for a toothless baby to mush up with their gums.
5 Wholemeal pasta shapes – easy to hold and to take bites from.
6 Banana – babies tend to love it, and it's easy to prepare and hold.
7 Casseroled beef and lamb – slow-cooked meat that breaks easily into moist strands is another iron-boosting food that baby can handle themselves.
8 Brown bread crust spread with nut butter – excellent nutritionally and very easy to hold and to practise chewing on.
9 Berries – whole strawberries, soft blackberries and raspberries, grapes torn in half, defrosted frozen blueberries, provide a fantastic range of shapes and flavours, great for babies practising a pincer grasp, and packed with goodness.
10 Apple or pear halves – great for teething babies.

Baby will be most comfortable in a highchair with a tray or pulled up to the table. Never feed them in anything but a fully upright position, and never leave them alone with food. Shape the food you get your baby into pieces that are easy for them to handle. Before they can pick up small bits, they will get on best with chip-shaped bits of food.

BLW is messy. Babies feeding themselves in our family wear big bibs with sleeves, or else nothing but a nappy. Even with a bib, often the food will get rubbed into the hair and ears. Regard it as just more good brain-training experience! We have a bucket one-third full of warm water ready for a super-quick bucket bath at the end of the meal, when things have got particularly messy. You may also need to wear an apron to lift your mucky baby out of the highchair when they are finished, if you want to keep your own clothes clean. It is worth choosing a hard plastic or wooden highchair instead of the padded kind, for ease of cleaning, and spreading newspaper or a plastic sheet under the chair, can help to protect the floor.

Manage mess, but don't try to avoid it

Some people advise against baby-led weaning because of the mess babies make when they feed themselves. But the only way to stop a baby making a mess at mealtimes is to hold their arms down while you spoon-feed – and that is a terrible waste of learning experience. The same, unfortunately, is true of most mess-saving parenting strategies: while baby is young, mess is an unavoidable by-product of good learning. Babies who are not allowed to make a mess will learn less.

Some toddlers with very tidy parents can learn to fear mess so much that they find it hard to play. In fact, even toddlers with relatively relaxed parents often develop 'neat freak' phases where they cannot bear even the chance of a spill or a smear, and this concern may be partly innate. It's good for babies to learn to be wary of dangerous mess like unidentified smears or overturned rubbish bins on the public pavement, but baby needs to feel relaxed about food and toy mess in their own home environment. Baby will feel relaxed if you do but, on the other hand, if you feel disturbed by mess on the inside, even while you allow baby free rein, they may pick up on your anxiety.

It can be very difficult to relax about mess, but to be a good brain trainer you do need to. This isn't to say you have to leave the mess where it is once baby has finished: babies need a certain amount of clear, tidy space to make their new messes in. They struggle to pick out interesting items from a pile of clutter. Prepare the area, and your storage systems, as well as you can to make clearing up easier. But then you need to relax and let the mess happen.

YOUR BABY'S FIRST MENU

When choosing first foods for your baby, you should consider three things:

1. Learning – Is it fun to eat? Does the food look, taste and smell interesting, and will it help your baby learn new skills with hands, fingers and mouth?
2. Variety – Are you building the range of foods to which your baby has been exposed? A varied diet should not only guard against allergy, but also add to the learning value of food, and guarantees the third objective:
3. Nutritional value – You should aim to make your baby's solid diet contain as wide a variety and as high a concentration of vitamins and minerals as breast milk. This will be very difficult, as breast milk is so nutritionally rich, but it should be the goal. In particular, think about the iron content of foods.

Baby cereal?

Most childcare books suggest that baby cereal should be the first thing on the menu. But cereal scores badly on our three criteria. It will be a few months before baby can feed themselves cereal – it won't even stick to a fist or a finger dipped into it like yogurt will – so you will have to spoon-feed. Cereal is not particularly interesting in taste or texture. It is naturally low in vitamins and minerals, but high in energy. If your baby eats a few tablespoons of cereal (most cereal packs suggest you make up such large amounts), they will have much less room for breast milk and a good variety of more valuable foods. Some cereal is fortified, which boosts its vitamin and mineral content, but if you want to use artificial vitamins and minerals as a back up to those that occur in food naturally, it makes more sense to give baby a supplement and leave room in their stomach for nutrient-rich foods.

Specific nutrients for building brains

SMART FATS

Brains are 60 per cent fat, so a baby with a rapidly growing brain needs an excellent supply of the right kinds of fat. The best kinds for brain building are long-chain polyunsaturated fatty acids, including omega 3 fats, EPA and DHA. Breast milk is an excellent source of these, as is oily fish. Some plant foods such as flax and rapeseed (canola) oil also contain omega 3s, but they are much less readily absorbed and used. Another important essential fatty acid is omega 6, found in nuts and seeds and meat. Omega 6 is much easier to come by, and most children eat too much omega 6 in proportion to the omega 3 they consume. Phospholipids are yet another sort of fatty acid used in the repair of brain cells and in the transmission of nerve impulses, and these are found in eggs, fish and soya.

A serving a week of oily fish will be good for your baby's brain, and you may also want to consider a fish oil supplement for young children once your baby has cut down on their consumption of breast milk.

THE SUNSHINE VITAMIN

While you are breastfeeding, provided your own diet is adequate, your baby should get all the vitamins and nutrients they need for their first six months, *with one exception*. There is one vitamin they may be short of before they even arrive in the world. Indeed, even on the most balanced diet, your baby may continue to be short of it after they move on to solids, and throughout their childhood and adulthood. And that shortage has been strongly linked not only with susceptibility to common viruses and cancers, but also to serious mental and neurological illnesses such as MS, depression and schizophrenia. This elusive vitamin is vitamin D.

The reason that your baby won't get enough vitamin D through your breast milk is not because breast milk is not a perfect food (fundamentally it is), but because diet is not a significant source of vitamin D. Our skin makes vitamin D on exposure to strong enough sunlight. And this is a problem, because we now know that too much sun exposure raises the risk of skin cancer.

Supplementation is a possible alternative, but here also things are not straightforward, because little is understood about the dosage required, as is illustrated by the fact that many scientists recommend taking the vitamin at a level significantly above the U.S. Tolerable Upper Intake Level. There is growing consensus that the daily levels recommended for supplementation in most countries may offer less than a fifth of what we need.

As a brain trainer, we would advise you to watch out for the latest information on vitamin D, as we do.

In the meantime, we would recommend:

▶ that you don't seek to protect your child from *all* summer sun exposure. Unfortunately, the gentle sun we get in Britain between October and March, on cloudy days, and in the early mornings and evenings, is no good for the making of vitamin D. If the sun is strong enough to make vitamin D, it is strong enough to burn. It is vitally important not to let your children burn their skin in the sun, but you might consider letting them play outdoors as near naked as possible and without sunscreen for *less than ten minutes* every sunny spring and summer day (a little longer only if they have dark skin). Their skin will stop making vitamin D after that point anyway, and they will be at risk of burning, so *never* leave it more than ten minutes. If it is too cool outside to run naked, you can put baby near an open door or under the shaft of light from an open window – for *less than ten minutes*.

▶ that you give your child a daily vitamin D supplement between the start of October and the end of March, and during prolonged periods of bad summer weather, from birth onwards. They need at least 400 IU (which is equivalent to 10 mcg – be careful not to mix up the two measurements scales, which are both commonly used). You might want to look at the evidence and the debate, and make your own decision on giving a higher dose than that. Some experts, (and also Oprah Winfrey!) recommend over 2,000 IU a day, especially for darker skinned people, but we cannot recommend that for children until there is more evidence on safety.

IRON

Another thing many children develop a shortage of in early childhood is iron. Iron is particularly important for myelination

76

and for the growth of the hippocampus. Iron deficiency can lead to developmental difficulties and mental damage, as well as other health problems and learning difficulties. And again, the picture of the problem, and possible solutions, is not very clear.

Breast milk contains modest amounts of highly absorbable iron. Baby will be born with iron reserves and should have plenty for their first six months. Although formula contains much more iron than breast milk, research has shown that breastfed babies nevertheless have better iron status at six months, perhaps because they absorb breast milk iron better, and do not lose blood through intestinal bleeding, as babies on formula do.

After six months, whether or not to give iron supplements is a highly debatable issue. Supplements may interfere with the absorption of the iron in breast milk, if baby is still breastfeeding. Some studies have shown that while iron supplements are very good insurance for populations of children at high risk of iron deficiency, they can actually make outcomes slightly *worse* for children who have good diets anyway.

On balance, the best solution seems to be to work on giving your child an iron-rich diet, and only to resort to supplements if it seems you are failing. Ideally, all children should be checked for iron deficiency before their first birthday (though in the UK they aren't). You could ask your doctor about this.

Meat is the best source of absorbable iron. Vegetables can contain lots, too, but it is much harder to absorb. Just a little meat with the vegetables will make it easier to absorb the iron from the vegetables. And the vitamin C in fruit and vegetables will help the absorption of iron from both the meat and the vegetables. Think as much about what *combinations* you serve, as about the individual foods.

One of the very best foods for your baby's iron status is liver. Calf's liver, chicken liver and lamb's liver are all good. Unfortunately, chemicals and other toxins can build up in liver, so only organic liver is safe for children to eat regularly. It is available for mail order on the internet, and you'll find that one pack in the freezer will go a long way. Babies do not share the prejudice against liver that many adults and older children have. Carefully braised fine liver slices are very easy to chew, or easily mashed for younger babies.

Some of the best vegetarian sources of iron are pumpkin seeds, dried apricots and prunes, and Popeye's old favourite, spinach.

ANTIOXIDANT VITAMINS A, C AND E

All these three vitamins help protect the brain from toxins, and all are found in a wide variety of fruits, vegetables and whole foods.

PHYTONUTRIENTS AND OTHER MIRACLE INGREDIENTS

There is growing evidence of the brain benefits to be had from a whole range of complex chemicals found in foods, from blueberries to beetroot. The headline message from all this research is that natural foods and the benefits we gain from them are very important but also very complicated indeed.

KEEP IT VARIED

It is almost impossible to remember what food includes which nutrient, and to design menus to include each one. There's no need to try. Science is only just beginning to discover the hidden benefits for health and brain development locked inside ordinary foods; we only know a tiny part of the story. Until we know much more, the best route to a healthy body and brain is to include as wide a range of 'whole foods' in the diet as possible. Whole foods are foods that retain a whole range of various nutrients that have not been 'stripped out' of the original plant parcel they came from, as sugar, white flour and vegetable fat have been. Include nuts, seeds, grains, poultry, red meat, seafood, and lots of fruit and vegetables, of as many different sorts as you can, in your child's diet. Choose foods that have plenty of taste and a wide range of bright colours: depth of flavour and colour are good signs that foods contain potent phytonutrients.

Babies don't like bland

People usually assume babies won't like foods with strong tastes. But this is more a self-fulfilling prophesy than a real fact. We have seen babies go crazy for dark chocolate, lemon, curry and non-alcoholic bitter. Many stronger-tasting foods are higher in nutrients than blander options, but if you get your baby used to mild-flavoured food they may get used to it and resist when you seek to widen their menu.

78

Foods to avoid

The best way to feel relaxed that your baby is getting a good brain training diet is not to count the portions of good things they eat, but to make sure that they eat very little that is bad or indifferent. If they don't have access to bad foods, research suggests they will be pretty good at balancing their own diet from the range of healthy choices on offer. Some foods are just not much good for your baby, and they should not be exposed to them too often. Others are positively bad for them, and you should try to avoid them in all but the most exceptional circumstances.

Here are the foods your child should really avoid:

TRANS FATS/HYDROGENATED FATS

These harmful substances are the product of fats and oils that have been altered chemically to prolong their shelf life. We have only recently begun to understand how they work in our bodies, and the list of the bad things they do to us grows longer and longer each year. The problems they cause may be to do with the fact that our bodies have difficulty getting rid of them once they've been absorbed, and with the fact that they block our bodies' use of other good fats.

It is essential that babies are able to use 'good' fats effectively to build their growing brains, and we do not yet know how much trans fats interfere with this process, though these fats have already been strongly linked to brain disease, as well as cancer, diabetes and infertility.

Trans fats and hydrogenated fats are found in many biscuits, cakes, margarine and fried products. Many supermarkets have removed these from their own-brand products. But remember, the other branded products these shops sell often still contain trans fats.

REFINED CARBOHYDRATE

The worst of these is sugar, but white bread and white pasta, white rice, and anything else made of white wheat, rice or other grain flour are almost as bad. Your baby's brain needs carbohydrate to give it energy to work, and they will crave carbohydrate-rich foods for this reason.

However, refined carbohydrate can be turned into energy too quickly, all at once. This will give your baby an energy buzz followed by a long slump. Although they may have eaten half their calories for the day, their brain will only be kept fed for half an hour. Children display swings in mood and behaviour if they eat foods that supply energy too quickly. This quick release of energy can also lead to diabetes and obesity.

The second problem with refined carbohydrate is that it contains nothing but energy. Babies do not need to consume many calories each day, and a single serving of refined carbohydrate may supply much of the energy they need. The problem is, the baby has not received any nutrients wrapped up with those calories, and they are 'empty'. There is less space in your baby's diet for nutrient-rich foods. When it comes to small tummies, you need to make every bite count.

The third problem with refined carbohydrates is that they are addictive. When we were hunter-gatherers, and struggled to find enough calories to get through the days, a tree that grew white bread would have been a great find. In those days, we ate more than enough nutrient-rich foods; finding the calorie-rich food was the problem. Babies can taste that sugar and white flour contain lots of energy for their brains, and love them for that reason. Increasingly large numbers of children grow to rely on the quick hit of energy they get from these refined foods. Some even develop phobias about non-refined, non-white foods.

For these reasons, you should keep refined carbohydrate out of the house. The occasional encounter with them will not do your child any harm, but they must not come to feel that they are available at home as an alternative to whole foods. You will save yourself a whole load of hassle in the long run if you can keep these off your baby's mental menu.

SWEET THINGS

Do everything you can to **keep the following foods well away from your baby** too:

- ▶ sweetened drinks
- ▶ artificial colourings
- ▶ sweets.

OCCASIONAL TREATS

Here are the foods that you should **keep out of your baby's sight, and out of your child's daily routines,** but which are not so bad as occasional treats:

- ▶ bread or pasta made wholly or partly with white flour
- ▶ preserved and processed meat
- ▶ sweetened yogurts
- ▶ ready meals (made without trans fats)
- ▶ cakes and biscuits (made without trans fats).

Other foods to avoid on general safety grounds

Salt – Your baby's kidneys can't cope with too much. Add the salt to your meal after you've given your baby their portion when you can. Carefully limit salty foods like processed meat and crisps.

Honey – Some honey contains traces of bacteria that cause botulism.

Nuts – Whole nuts are unsuitable for young children because of the risk of choking. Peanuts, even chopped, pose a particular risk because they can irritate the lungs if inhaled. Peanut butter should always be spread thinly.

Shark, swordfish, marlin – Such big fish concentrate heavy metals in their bodies, which can endanger your child's brain development.

Cow's milk – Not suitable as a drink until after they reach 12 months.

Eggs – A great food for babies, with lots of iron, but egg white is a common allergen in very young babies. Do not introduce it until after six months, and wait longer if there is a history of egg allergy in the babies in your family.

Tips for successful brain-building meals

Once you know all there is to know about the perfect brain-building diet, there's still one problem – you can put a baby in a highchair, but you can't make them eat. Remember that as long as your baby is breastfeeding, all they really *need* to eat are some high-iron foods from time to time. Mostly, eating is about play, learning, and practice for the future. Here are some top tips for making it likely that you will get a balanced meal into your baby:

- ▶ **Make eating a social occasion** – Societies all over the world throughout history have used meals as an opportunity for chat and social bonding. Let your baby eat at the table with the rest of the family as often as you can. They will have the opportunity to watch you eat and to copy you, they will associate eating with the pleasures of sociability, and they will get a master class in conversation skills at the same time.
- ▶ **Eat well yourself** – Baby will want to eat what you eat. If you eat less well than you think they should, you are making trouble for yourself.
- ▶ **Get the order right** – Some babies tend to go for bread, potatoes, pasta or rice first, and eat so much that they have no room for fruit, vegetables and protein. If this happens, put the blueberries, fish, broccoli or whatever in front of your baby first, while they are hungry.
- ▶ **Convey a positive attitude to healthy foods** – Never let your baby see you pull a 'yuck' face or say anything that implies that it is a chore to eat healthy foods, or that you would rather stick to chips and ice cream if you could. Try to let them see you enjoy healthy foods.
- ▶ **Use good role models** – As baby gets older, seeing other people, and particularly other children, eating becomes extremely motivating. Let your baby watch you, their older siblings, cousins or friends eating healthily whenever you can.
- ▶ **Talk about food** – Name it, talk about how it looks and how it tastes, and how good it is for you all. Baby will learn a lot at mealtime, and become interested in food.

Top ten tips for reading labels

1 **Ingredients that end with "ose' are almost always a type of sugar,** except sucralose, which is an artificial sweetener. Baby can do without added refined sugar of any kind. Fructose and lactose are less bad for baby's teeth than glucose, but still not a good addition to any food.

2 **Baby food needs a label check too.** It seems shocking, but even foods for the youngest babies often have sugar, white flour and bad fats added to them. Rusks are often particularly unhealthy. There are excellent baby foods available that are made with organic fruit, vegetables, meat or fish. Choose one of those.

3 **Avoid products with a string of E numbers,** or many ingredients you would not have in your own kitchen. Not all E numbers are equally bad. Some common store cupboard ingredients like baking soda have E numbers, as do natural colours and vitamin C. But, knowing that customers will prefer the sound of 'vitamin C' to 'E300', usually producers use the common name rather than the number, if the ingredient is something innocent.

4 **Look carefully at juice.** Babies shouldn't drink too much juice, but a little bit can be a good addition to their diet as they grow. Anything labelled 'juice *drink*' is not pure juice but is sweetened with sugar or artificial sweetener. Some leading brands of 'juice drink' even contain hydrogenated vegetable oil. It's best for your baby to drink juices from a wide range of different fruits. Children are often given cordial and squash, but these contain either sugar or artificial sweetener.

5 **Beware the small print behind reassuring labels.** Don't assume that because a product boasts one health claim, you can trust it to avoid other bad ingredients. Products can be labelled 'low fat', 'light', 'organic', 'lower in salt and sugar', 'wholewheat', 'high in fibre', and still be terrible for your baby. Note, 'low fat' dairy products are not suitable for babies and should not be given to them in their first year.

6 **For children, the amount of fat is less important than the type of fat.** Hydrogenated fat is the real baddy, saturated fat is not great, but polyunsaturated and monounsaturated fats are by and large okay. Olive oil, safflower oil and rapeseed oil are better than palm oil, sunflower oil, suet and lard.

7 **No bran for babies.** While whole grains are good for your baby, products that concentrate bran, the fibrous bits of grain, will fill them up too much, leaving less room for nutrients.

8 **Check the ingredients of your daily bread.** While bread is rarely terribly unhealthy, because we eat a lot of it, it's important to choose the right loaf. You should choose wholemeal bread – which isn't necessarily the same as brown. Lots of brown bread contains more than 50 per cent white flour, which is often called 'wheat flour' on the label. Make sure wholewheat flour is the only wheat flour listed, and that there is no added sugar. Rye, wholemeal spelt, corn and seeds are nutritious additions.

9 **Don't rely on brands** – make your own judgement. Products marketed under brands or names associated with healthy eating – such as Annabel Karmel – may still contain sugar or white flour. Cheaper unbranded alternatives may have healthier ingredients. Judge for yourself.

10 **Check your breakfast cereal.** Lots of breakfast cereals carry health messages on the box, but very few of them are really fit for your baby or young child to eat. Most are packed with salt, sugar and refined carbohydrate. Choose muesli, cornflakes, or shredded or puffed whole grains, but check the label to avoid added sugar. Remember that babies don't have to have either baby or grown-up cereal for breakfast. You can give them curry or pizza, they won't mind a bit.

What, no treats?

Cutting sugar out of your child's daily diet might seem too much like spoiling their fun. Luckily there is an alternative, all-natural sweetener that releases energy to their brain nice and slowly, has a range of other health benefits, and is positively good for their teeth. Xylitol is found in many fruits and vegetables and is usually produced from birch or maize. It can be used instead of sugar in any ordinary recipe for cakes, cookies, ice-cream, etc (though it's no good for baking dough with yeast). A chocolate cake made with cocoa, xylitol, lots of eggs, and wholegrain flour or almond meal will be positively great for your little one's health, as well as delicious. You can also buy sweets and chocolate made of xylitol on the internet.

Shopping list for smart store-cupboard and freezer snacks

Your baby needs lots of fresh and freshly cooked food to feed their growing brain, but good food doesn't have to be difficult. There are also plenty of easy to prepare snacks that you can keep in stock in the store cupboard and freezer.

▶ Nut butters – almond, hazelnut, brazil and cashew. These are readily available, popular with children, and are an excellent source of protein. They contain a wider range of nutrients, and a better balance of fats, than peanut butter.

▶ Wholemeal pitta bread – vacuum packs last up to a month in the cupboard, and longer in the freezer. Split into pockets, pitta makes nice thin neat sandwiches easy for young children to manage, and which do not spray crumbs like ordinary bread.

▶ Tinned sardines or mackerel – excellent source of omega 3s and calcium, usually popular with children.

▶ Mayonnaise made with olive, rapeseed, or another healthy oil, and without sugar – mix with yogurt and use as a dip for sticks of cucumber, broccoli, carrots or other vegetable.

▶ Pumpkin-seed spread – like nut-butter, but with higher iron content. One of the best vegetarian sources of iron.

▶ Oatcakes made with olive oil (not palm oil, suet or 'vegetable fat') – oats are a healthy alternative to wheat, and oatcakes offer an energy-rich snack, either by themselves or topped with a dollop of cream cheese, hummus, nut or seed butter, or mashed avocado or banana.

▶ Frozen berries – berries are a super food, and frozen packs of mixed berries are a cheap and convenient way of getting a wide range of phytonutrients into your child. Defrost in the microwave or pour over some boiling water to soften them up, or blend them in their frozen state with a banana, milk, soya, yoghurt or fruit juice to make an instant ice cream or smoothie.

▶ 'Steam packs' of ready-prepared vegetables to cook in the microwave – a handy way of serving your children a range of vegetables all at once, ready cut into manageable pieces, and cooked until they're soft enough to eat. Some babies like a drizzle of olive oil on them, or a mayonnaise and yogurt dip.

- ▶ Rice cakes made with brown rice – another healthy change from wheat bread.
- ▶ Tinned hummus.
- ▶ Tinned mixed beans, canned without sugar.

YOUR TURN

▶ Breastfeed your baby, if you can, for as long as you can.

▶ Breastfeed your baby whenever they seem to want to.

▶ Don't be inhibited about breastfeeding in public places.

▶ Don't introduce solid foods until six months.

▶ Introduce wheat soon after your baby turns six months.

▶ Let your baby feed themselves a wide, interesting and nutritious range of solid foods.

▶ Make sure your baby gets enough vitamin D, from the sun or from supplements.

▶ Feed your baby plenty of iron-rich foods.

▶ Ensure they get lots of other vitamins and nutrients by offering a wide diet of whole foods.

▶ Keep foods containing hydrogenated fats and refined carbohydrate out of your baby's sight.

▶ Make sure you have a stock of handy nutritious snacks in your cupboard and freezer so that you do not have to choose between nutrition and convenience.

6

....

Bringing things together: brain training between three and eight months

In this chapter you will learn:
- *how to help your baby get the most out of playing with things*
- *how to join and encourage your baby in active play*
- *how to make and choose suitable toys*
- *how to create an environment that helps your baby learn.*

During these months, your baby will really get into physical play, beginning with the sort of material experimentation that will be second nature to them throughout early childhood.

Baby moves from batting, grabbing, holding and waving to dropping, stretching and banging. They learn to control their body, first mastering big movements like accurate swiping, and then moving on to fine motor skills like picking up small objects between finger and thumb. These new abilities allow them to learn about the physical world and to build on their innate intuitions about physical forces like gravity and acceleration, and space and extension.

They also allow them to act on the world in a whole range of ways. Baby is no longer a spectator but part of the action. The feeling of control is a vital part of learning. Babies want to understand their world so that they can change it. Knowing is tied up with wanting, needing, and doing. Motivation is a keystone of learning.

Key skills, in the order they develop, and how to help

BABY HOLDS HEAD UP AND HAS GOOD NECK CONTROL

Your baby does 'push ups' on their tummy to look around. They may rock on their tummy, waving arms and legs. If they spend a good bit of time on their stomach, they will soon learn to roll over. Let your baby spend as much time on their tummy as they are happy with, and also sit them more upright in a baby seat when they are awake. They may start to stretch their neck to grab and suck their own feet.

BABY IS ABLE TO GRASP AN OBJECT ON PURPOSE

Baby was born with the reflex to grasp anything placed in their palm. Now they can actually reach out and grab things. At first baby will reach with both arms and 'gather' a dangled toy towards their body. Next they will reach with one hand, using their hand as though they were wearing a mitten, to grasp an object between thumb and palm and fingers. Your baby's aim will improve until they are accurate at reaching even for a slowly moving object. They will learn to adjust the shape of their hand to the shape of the object they are reaching for, and to pass a toy from hand to hand. Soon they will practise grabbing skills on your glasses, nose and hair – ouch!

Research shows that the age at which your baby manages these tasks has a lot to do with the opportunities around for practice. Babies who are given few suitable objects to reach for may take twice as long to reach this milestone as babies with good opportunities. In one experiment, researchers made mittens out of velcro for three-month-olds, to give them an edge in grabbing fluffy toys. Sure enough, these babies were extra good at reaching and grabbing a month later. You could try sticking velcro to some scratch mitts and dangling small balls of wool for baby to reach out for. Or just **make a point of holding out easily grabbable and interesting toys** to your baby as often as you can, or set up a play area where interesting toys are just within reach.

In the latter part of this period, your baby will begin to work on picking up small things: Raking items towards themselves and struggling to pick them up with their whole hand at first, later beginning to use their first finger and thumb.

Once your baby has perfected their ability to get hold of things, they may start to do things with them. Energetic waving comes first, followed by banging and then dropping and aimless throwing. Releasing an object is actually a difficult skill for your baby to learn. They will be very pleased with themselves when they learn to drive you crazy by dropping from the high chair every toy you give them to play with.

BABY'S PERCEPTIONS MATURE

Soon, your baby will seem to react to sights and sounds as though their perceptions were just like an adult's. They can track a bird or butterfly as it flies down the other side of the street. Their depth perception improves, as they demonstrate through accurate reaching. They gaze intently and can spot the tiniest objects to poke at. They reliably turn towards sounds.

BABY KNOWS WHAT TO EXPECT

By now, baby is getting on top of their world. Bedtime and nap time become more and more predictable. You'll know better what to expect. Their body language becomes more organized, and some of it seems to be directed right at you. Your baby develops a particular noise and way of waving their arms when they want to be picked up, or for you to come down and play with them. And they also know what to expect from you. When you sit them on your knee in a particular position they look pleased and excited because they know some milk is coming their way. When you sit them in their pushchair they no longer struggle to get out, because now they expect a fun outing to follow. Towards the end of this period, you may notice that your baby seems to understand a few words, especially if they appear in a particular context. Try asking them, 'Where's Daddy,' and they may turn in his direction. Certainly they know their own name, responding consistently when you call them.

BABY LEARNS TO SIT AND PLAY

Once baby can sit up with some support, they can manipulate objects more freely, as well as look around at the action and chat and wave arms at you from across the room.

THE SOUNDS BABY MAKES BECOME MORE VARIED, AND THEY BEGIN TO PLAY WITH SOUND

At the start of this period, baby will make mainly vowel sounds like 'ahh', and 'oooh'. Soon you will notice them playing with their mouth, making clicking, popping and bubbling noises. By the end of the period, and sometimes as early as six months, baby will be stringing vowels and consonants into long strings – 'babababa'. Encourage this experimentation with sound by asking baby to copy the noises you make, and by copying them in turn. Baby will be fascinated by non-language noises, like the noise you make for a car or plane, or animal noises. Watch them look at your mouth when you make a clip-clop noise, for example.

BABY WORKS ON THEIR MOBILITY

Babies vary widely in terms of the progress they make on mobility during this period. Some babies roll over in the direction they would like to travel, others dig in their toes to move forward on their tummies, or use their arms to pull themselves forward. Others lean forward from a sitting position onto their hands to make a bridge, and from that position learn to crawl. Some babies combat-crawl, with their stomachs on the floor, others quickly progress to true crawling (or creeping as it is sometimes called), on knees and hands. Cross crawling is the most efficient sort of crawling – this is when baby moves one arm and the leg on the opposite side forward and then moves forward the other arm and leg, alternately. Try to crawl yourself, and you will find you don't cross crawl. Your baby will soon be better at it than you are!

Other babies still find it difficult to get around on their own, even by the end of this period. If so, they will almost certainly enjoy moving with your help. Hold baby's hands so that they can walk along, or offer your fingers for them to pull themselves forward by, when they are on their stomach.

Training tips for this age range

KEEP UP A FLOW OF THINGS

At this age babies become insatiable consumers of stuff. They are keen to hold and suck as many different things as they can get their hands on. But they do have to be *different*. No matter how well-designed or 'stimulating' the toys you buy for your baby, or how many you buy, they will quickly be bored with them and want new things to get hold of. Babies have a surprisingly good memory by this age. They recognize, and therefore often reject, toys they have already explored. If your baby is crying and seemingly uninterested in everything you offer them to play with, try an object they have never seen before. The kitchen is a good source of safe and interesting objects: babies love things made of wood, silicone and metal, so wooden spoons, whisks and tea-strainers can appeal more than most ordinary toys. But watch out for sharp points.

A fun and easy way to pass the time is to take your baby in their pram to a big toyshop or department store. You can hand them an endless flow of unfamiliar objects to try out, and they will get the benefit of exploring a lot of toys in a fun environment even if you don't buy a thing.

LEARN TO PLAY ALONG WITH BABY

When your baby was younger, playing with them meant doing things while they watched. This age sees the beginning of play in which you and your baby take part together. Now you need to develop brain training play skills that will be important to your interactions with your baby for many years to come.

Playing with young children is a delicate mixture of demonstration and supervision, of helping and standing aside to watch. Your baby learns most when they have a playmate who understands just what they are capable of, and can organize activities that stretch their new skills without making them switch off with frustration. At this age, your job is to do simple things like hold up, move, or bring close toys for your baby to grab, help them to sit up, and so on. But you need to be sensitive to their abilities if they are to get the most out of your play sessions. Keep asking yourself, 'Can my baby do *this* yet?', and put them to the test, whether it's catching at a toy as you move it past them, or squeezing the tummy of a squeak toy. If your baby is not managing to pass most of the tests you set them, or is showing signs of frustration very soon after you start to play, you may be pushing too hard. Interestingly, research shows that mothers and fathers tend, on average, to play differently with their babies. Mothers have a lower threshold for intervening when their baby is having difficulty with a task than fathers, who often wait longer to see whether their baby can manage by themselves. This contrast in brain training styles is probably good for your baby, so try to let your partner play with baby in the way that comes most naturally, without trying to impose your own standards. But keep your partner and other people who play with baby up-to-date with what they can do. 'You know, he can rock to and fro on all fours now,' 'Yesterday he picked up about ten peas one by one with no trouble at all'.

LET BABY CALL THE SHOTS

During this period, your baby will start showing very clear personal preferences and interests. No matter how odd your own baby's obsessions, try to indulge them. Research shows that babies learn more quickly if their carers talk to them about the things they themselves choose to look at, rather than attempting to divert their attention to other more 'interesting' things. Of course, when baby is at a loose end it's your job to draw their attention to remarkable sights. But don't feel you need to cut across what seems baby's almost crazy obsession with taps, shoelaces, or whatever.

Insight: odd obsessions

From four months, Tass would squeal whenever we passed a hook or other dangly metal thing, and wave his arms until we took him over to pull at it and coo. Peacocks and peacock feathers also make him squeak with joy. Outings are made interesting by looking out for such objects.

Ten tips for buying and organizing brain-training toys

Choose toys without one 'right' way to play. Young children do not like to play with toys the way they are 'supposed' to be played with. They like to use skittles as microphones, stacking rings as hammers, and so on. This innovative sort of play is better for their brains, and a more impressive display of intelligence than simple rule-following.

Choose toys made of various materials and textures. Babies are very alert to what toys are made of. It can sometimes seem that a singing ball made of plastic is not really interestingly different from a plastic play desk, from their point of view. But introduce some mossy twigs from the garden, and they will perk up and take interest. Look out for toys and household objects with really striking tactile qualities: an old rubber tricycle wheel, a coconut, a feather boa.

Wood, metal, ceramic and stone are always favourites. Unlike plastic, natural materials vary in temperature, smell, taste, and the sounds they make when banged together. Babies really notice this, and if all their toys are plastic, will become obsessed with your house keys and your wooden spoons.

Vary the scale of the toys. Some toys should be big, like a beach ball, to encourage gross motor skills; others medium, like stacking cups; and others small, like paper stars or threadable cotton reels, to encourage finger and eye coordination.

Establish a system of rotation. You will find that baby gets sick of toys just by having them within their field of vision, even if they never play with them. Put them out of sight for a month and then bring them back out, and they will be as exciting as they were when new. Try storing your toys in three or four separate boxes. Each week, bring out a different box and spread out the toys within baby's reach. Keep the other boxes out of sight until a change is needed.

Buy ahead of time. Some of the best toys can do double duty, as a tactile toy for a younger baby, and then as a more structured activity for an older child. Baby may enjoy the chunky pieces and bold pictures on a wooden farm animal shape puzzle even when they are only a few months old, then learn some animal words from it between six and 12 months, and then be able to do the puzzle in their second year.

Avoid electronic toys that encourage passivity. By the end of their first couple of months, baby needs toys they can fully interact with and 'work' on. They will probably have little interest in any toy that they can't manipulate, and it is not good for them to spend too much time gazing passively even at the most 'stimulating' electronic mobile or the like.

Choose toys that help baby with their most recent developmental goals. Watch for cues. Does baby enjoy pulling on lamp cables?

Putting peas in their drinking cup? Balancing their beaker on top of their cereal bowl? They might enjoy pull-along toys, a box with shells to put inside it, or bricks to build with.

Limit the number of soft toys. Baby will only be interested in these if you both together can give them each a particular identity and this will be hard work if there are dozens of them competing for attention. Bear in mind, too, that if asthma runs in the family, washable soft toys are best.

Check the material of any toy that baby regularly sucks on. Don't let them suck for extended periods on anything made of plastic or vinyl. These materials may leech harmful chemicals that could harm their brain. Also think about where you bought anything painted or dyed. If it did not come from a well-established children's store or company, the paints might contain lead or other harmful substances.

DESIGNING BABY HOUSE WALKS

We know that adults find it easier to memorize information if they can associate it with physical space, and the same may be true of babies. Certainly by the time baby is three months old, and maybe much sooner, they will love touring the house, going from one room to another, looking at the sights to be seen in each, and listening to your commentary, which will soon develop into as catchy a patter as you'll get from the most professional tour guide. A predictable movement from room to room, accompanied by a predictable stream of language, will help baby find the patterns in their world, and set them off towards comprehension of their first words. Right now Tass goes into a frenzy of excitement when we take him on his tour. He reaches out for each 'sight' and smiles and coos as if it were an old friend. Interestingly, his excitement seems to be triggered by our naming of the sights, rather than by seeing the things themselves, as though he is thrilled that he is beginning to be able to put sounds and sights together.

Here are two ideas for tours; ideally you could combine both on one walk. Many babies who like physical play nevertheless tire of each play session quite quickly, getting frustrated with you or their toys. If your baby does this, those moments of frustration are the perfect time to take them on a tour. As you tour the house, try to visit each sight in the same order each time. Baby will enjoy anticipating what comes next. Soon you will see their eyes go towards the next stop ahead of you.

BABY SAFARI

You will find it easier to chat to your baby if there are simple pictures of things around for you to draw to their attention, and soon your baby will be starting to learn their names. Pictures of animals are particularly fun, because you can also make noises and actions to go with each one. Flowers and vehicles are also good.

Some of the ornaments you already have up may be baby-friendly. Seek out bold, bright pictures or figures. Check your possessions: books, clothes, mugs, bags, blankets, cushions. Are there bold, recognizable pictures on any of them? The more assorted the objects you can find that display interesting pictures, the better – baby will have a nice range of different sorts of pictures to look at, and different things to touch. If you already have a collection of soft toys, hide some of the more striking ones inside cupboards or behind curtains, ready to jump out. If you are falling short, check through magazines and pull out a few big bold graphics.

Then you can design your tour. In each room of the house, set up a few sights for baby. These needn't dominate your décor, they might even be hard for visitors to notice. Bring the jacket with the tiger on the back to the front of the coat rack, keep the mug with the Dalmatian on the kitchen windowsill, make sure the postcard with the sunflower does not get covered over on the pin board, hang the fish-shaped bath mitt on the back of the bathroom door. If you are going to stick up a few extra images, do so at the height you hold baby, so you can both see comfortably.

MULTI-SENSE TOUR

Especially when your baby is younger, they will particularly enjoy exercising all their senses on their strolls around the house. Make sure that your routine includes something exciting to touch, smell, taste and hear, as well as see. Keep a pot of basil or other herb on a windowsill, and let your baby sniff as you pass – you could even let them grab and chew a leaf once they are old enough to try. Stick a peacock or ostrich feather somewhere at baby level, and use it to tickle their face and tummy whenever you go by. Look out for some sturdy wind chimes you can let them bat at. Buy a couple of cellophane-wrapped bars of natural soap, and let your baby hold and smell. Hang a velvety scarf somewhere up high, for baby to burrow their forehead into. If your windows are double glazed and safe, let your baby press their cheek against the cold glass. Run water from the cold tap over the tips of their toes. Let them smell the fruit in the fruit bowl. If you have a garden, let them smell every flower, as well as the spicy sent of a conifer bush, and the green smell of the cut grass in the compost. Your baby will love to watch and feel the wind stirring the leaves, and the way beads of dew or rain on a leaf run together when you move it, or sparkle on a spider web when you blow. Babies love the sound of drips, and of water going down a drain.

Too soon for television

We deal with television in-depth only in our final chapter, because the message from most experts on television for children under two is simple: they shouldn't watch any. Having said that, there is no evidence – and it seems unlikely – that very occasional television watching (say once a month when baby is sick or parents are having a crisis) will do much harm.

YOUR TURN

▶ Now that your baby's senses have matured, take them out and about to see the sights.

▶ At home, keep your baby supplied with a stream of new and interesting things.

▶ Develop a system for selecting and managing their growing collection of toys.

▶ Practise playing with your baby, encouraging and helping along their exploration of objects.

▶ Spend lots of time carrying your baby around and pointing out things of interest, inside and outside the house.

▶ Whenever you can, immerse yourself and your baby in the vivid world of sights, smells and sounds, and provide a running commentary as you do so.

7

Learning language: building the foundations

In this chapter you will learn:
- *how babies start to understand language*
- *how babies move towards speech*
- *other important steps forward in communication*
- *how to use baby signs.*

It's hard to grasp the size of the task ahead of the pre-verbal human baby. Language comes so naturally to us that we lose sight of what a huge achievement it is. Language will change the way your baby relates to the world completely, as well as letting them share new forms of closeness with the people in it.

It's easy to think of language simply as a matter of labels that go with particular items. But there are several stages babies need to go through before they can match up things and words in this way, and if you understand them, you can help. In fact, if you or other people don't help, your baby will not learn language. Even if they could watch television all day, a baby cannot learn language unless people around them talk to them. If a baby does not learn language when they are young, their brain will change and their language may never develop normally.

Comprehension comes first

Every day, for the three months since he was born, Brigid has shown baby Tass the car before he got into it, and named it. Surely by now Tass should have caught on to the simple fact that the little sound 'car' stands for the big loud thing he travels in?

But consider what Tass actually hears. As he leaves the house each morning, Brigid says 'heybabytassykinsshallwegetinthecar?nowwheresthecar?' Even if Tass can spot the word 'car' in the flow of words, he still needs to figure out that 'car' as mum says it today in her cheeriest voice is the same word as 'car' as she said it yesterday feeling very tired, and the same word as his grandfather Fergus says with his deeper tones and Irish twang.

Young babies are extremely sensitive to language sounds – much more sensitive than adults are. You can play a baby two very similar language sounds and they will notice that they are different, while to an adult they will sound the same.

This is because to learn a language we need to pay attention only to relevant differences in sound. We need to learn what range of sounds count, in our particular language, as the building blocks of words.

For example, in Japanese, the difference between the sounds that in English are made by the letters 'l' and 'r' is not relevant. In Japanese, both these sounds count as one. Japanese adults cannot hear any difference between 'l' and 'r' at all. Similarly, in Thai there are two relevantly different language sounds, both of which an English speaker would hear as 'p'. Adult language speakers have learned *not* to pay any attention to differences in sound that are not relevant to meaning in their native language. Japanese babies under nine months old can hear the difference between 'r' and 'l' perfectly well. But this sensitivity to all the subtle differences in language sounds makes it much harder for babies to pick out words in the language stream, because no two 'l' or 'r' sounds are ever exactly the same. Towards the end of the first year, as babies are beginning to understand words, they begin to lose interest in sound differences that are not relevant to meaning in their language.

Then there's the business of figuring out where one phrase, and then one word, ends and the next begins – how to break things up when mum says 'heybabytassykinshallwegetinthecar?nowwheres thecar?' To do this, baby's brain works as a powerful calculator, processing the frequency of thousands of different noises and noise combinations they hear in the language around them. Baby will notice what sound combinations are allowed within a word in their language. They will notice that, in English, for example, 'pv' is a very unusual combination within a word, so if mum says 'stopvan' there is a clue to where to break up the words. Patterns of stress and intonation provide more clues.

Once baby has identified language sounds, phrases and words, and distinguishes them as they come across them, they need to figure out how to attach them to things in the world. This is hard work too. In a way, though, the most amazing thing is that it ever occurs to baby to try to match sound-symbols with things in the world at all. Their brain is pre-programmed to work at this task, and to search for patterns in the world to help them.

When you say to your baby, 'Look, there's a bird', there will usually be dozens of items around to which they might attach the word 'bird': a tree, a cloud, the window frame, the wind, the cold, the smell of the toast burning. If your baby is quicker to notice the clouds of smoke coming from the toaster than you are, and they are mainly thinking about that as you go on and on about the bird, it would make sense for them to attach the word 'bird' to the idea of burning toast.

One helpful and significant step in the right direction when it comes to attaching words to things in the world is the ability to follow the direction of a pointed finger. This is a difficult skill – something that animals do not learn. During their first half-year, notice how your baby looks not in the direction you are pointing but rather in at your hand itself. Parents often snap their fingers or tap on the object being indicated to get baby to look at the topic of conversation. Eventually they will notice that looking beyond your pointing hand is usually interesting. Sometime in the next six months they will learn to follow your point.

Research shows that babies are much more likely to attach a word to a thing if the thing named is *moving*. For this reason 'dog', 'car', and 'big sister' are all good bets for early topics of conversation. Do your best, when you are naming things for your baby, to make sure you are both paying attention to the same thing: if your baby is already looking at something you can tell them about, label that object first. Draw their attention to things by tapping them, moving them, lifting your baby right up close, or waiting until they move or make a noise, until your baby is willing and able to follow your points.

Their own name is also likely to be one of the first words your baby recognizes, though at first they may not really understand that it stands for themselves, but rather view it as a sound-sign that means something like 'Look at mum for some fun!' During your baby's first half year, you can occasionally test to see if baby seems to know their own name, and also get an insight into how babies process sound patterns to sort out words.

Start out by calling your baby's name. Do they turn to look? Now try calling another name, with a different stress pattern. So if your baby is named *Ru*by, try calling '*Diane*'! If she still turns to look, she may just be reacting to the animated, 'calling' cadence of your voice. If she does not turn to look when you call a name with a different stress pattern, try another name with the same stress pattern as her own. Does baby *Ru*by also answer to '*Sa*rah'? Does *Diane* also turn around when you call her '*Marie*'? When your baby is turning around only when you call their own name, and not names with similar stress patterns, they have made a lot of progress processing language sounds.

The names of family members may be some of the earliest words baby gets to understand. Around the table, try out the 'where's daddy?' game. Go through each person at the table, asking baby, 'Where's X?', and watching to see if they turn in the right direction. Baby will love to see the look of pride and joy on the face of each relative as they show they have learned their name!

If you have set up baby house walks as we suggest in Chapter 6, you may also notice that baby gets to know the names of the things on the walk pretty early on. Their eyes may turn in the direction of the next thing on the tour if you name it before you get there. To test their knowledge, try subtly changing the order you visit the sights, but announcing what you will be looking at next before you move towards it. Can your baby anticipate the direction you'll take with the angle of their head and body?

At six months or after, baby may show clear signs of understanding a few favourite words. Baby Tass, now nine months, has known the word 'peacock' for a few months now. If we show him a picture or a figure of a peacock, or a peacock's feather when we're out and about, he will look at it with interest – but as soon as we say the word 'peacock', pleasure spreads across his face and he will grin, as though he's delighted to have made a little bit of sense. Look out for those magical 'light bulb' moments, when you can almost see a flash of magic as your baby grasps their first bits of language. The radiant joy of their smile when they understand your words will make you believe, if you didn't before, that babies love to learn.

To help build the number of comprehended words, **we need to talk to our babies** – and talk, and talk. There is a strong correlation between the size of baby's spoken and comprehended vocabularies and the amount of language addressed to them. Language addressed to others, or coming out of a television or radio, does not boost a baby's vocabulary in the same way.

This is partly because the manner in which we instinctively talk to babies plays an important role in helping to boost their language learning. Since your baby's birth, you will have been talking to them in what researchers call 'motherese'. This baby talk is the way that people in all cultures tend to talk to babies. It is higher and more variably pitched, and is slower, simpler, more rhythmic, and contains more emphases than normal speech. Not just mothers, but also fathers and other care-givers, even children, speak to babies like this. Funnily enough, men tend to think that they don't use motherese, even when it can be shown that they really do. As babies get to the stage when they are clearly learning to understand words, care-givers in all cultures tend to emphasize and repeat new words when they arise, placing them at the end of sentences even when it makes no grammatical sense to do so. 'Look, there's a RABBIT under the hat, a RABBIT! Look at that naughty little RABBIT there – yes, it's a RABBIT.' Don't be inhibited about talking to your baby in a 'silly' voice, or about following your own instinctive language-teaching methods. Go with what comes naturally. Research shows that motherese really does help babies learn language. Indeed, some research has shown that babies under two can *only* learn new words if they are 'taught' them in motherese. All this provides a clue to why it is important for babies not only to hear language around them, but also to have engaged carers talking directly to them.

Does 'motherese' help your baby to learn?

Introduce your baby to two new objects they have never encountered before, such as, for example, a cotton reel and a kiwi fruit (which you could just call a 'reel' and 'kiwi' to make it easier). Name one for them in animated motherese, repeating the name as often as you like. Then explain the name of the other item to them in the sort of voice you would use if you were

(Contd)

speaking to an adult. Later on, put the two objects in front of your baby among a few other toys, and ask them 'Where's the kiwi?' Then ask them, 'Where's the reel?' Are they more successful at picking out the object you named in motherese? If they cannot pick out either first time, keep naming one in motherese for them and the other in normal language, and see which word they learn first.

At this stage, baby will love to have **you label everything in their environment.** They will enjoy being carried around an ordinary boring room, with you going, 'It's a *cup*, *cup*, yes, it's a *blue cup*. Now, there's the window – look, there are some cows, *cows*,' and so on, for as long as you can keep it up. By the time they are past their first birthday, and perhaps well before, they will be starting to understand simple sentences or word combinations, so you can also model and repeat these for them too: 'It's a blue cup', 'Now the *cow has gone – where's the cow*?'.

After your baby has learned to recognize a word, they will be able to spot it in general conversation. From time to time you may notice your baby staring intently and excitedly at your face as you chat to another adult. Most likely you've just mentioned the word 'helicopter', 'kangaroo', or something else they have recently learned, and they are waiting for you to repeat it.

Now is the time to **introduce your baby to books,** if you haven't done so already. Picture books are a great way of broadening the conversation with your baby, and are also a great way of keeping a mobile baby still for a few minutes! Early on, baby may particularly enjoy books with a realistic image on each page of just one thing, which you can name for them.

Books of **nursery rhymes will also be particularly useful for language development,** as well as a popular choice with most babies. Rhyme and rhythm help babies to find the patterns in language.

When you read to your baby, don't feel you must stick to the words on the page. These may not include the special, infant-directed patterns that you will naturally want to use when speaking to your baby. When baby is young, they will get most from books if you talk a lot about the pictures and re-phrase and repeat the meaning of words on the page.

Joining the conversation

Apart from understanding you, the other thing that makes babies happy is to know that you understand them. Since birth you have fed your baby's sense of security by coming running whenever they cry. But now they want to give you more detailed orders, and, more excitingly still, share thoughts with you.

Here are some of the tricks baby will use to get their message across.

EYE CONTACT

Many brain trainers find their baby's attempts to catch their eye pretty exciting. Baby will look intently at you, staring right at your eyes, until you look – then, typically, they continue to stare, maybe giving an 'eh, eh' or other 'help!' sound. Then they may look towards whatever they want, or they may even point. These attempts to make eye contact are significant, because they tell you that baby now understand a bit about how people work. You press a button if you want your play table to play you a song, but if you want dad to do something, you need to get his attention – you need to get him on your wavelength. Baby already understands, if only implicitly, that other people think and feel just like they do.

POINTING

Babies are working on their point from the early weeks onwards. At first baby will point with their whole arm, next with a whole hand of outstretched fingers, before settling finally on the mature forefinger point. Early points are not an attempt at communication, but rather part of the way baby directs their own attention towards whatever they are interested in. Their first successful points, which really direct your attention, may be a lucky combination of intentional eye-contact with a point that's still really for their own benefit.

SIGNS

By nine months, baby may also use sounds and gestures, if not conventional spoken words, to get their point across. Most babies start to clap around eight months. They may join in delightedly when others clap, or, sometimes, give themselves a clap and look around at the audience when they do something clever, hoping to trigger applause from everyone else. Baby may start to wave goodbye sometime around nine months. And, around this age, many babies begin to copy animal noises you have told them about.

Some babies are absolutely thrilled when, by making a mooing noise for cow, or popping their lips for fish, they manage to draw your attention to what they're looking at, and to let you know what's on their minds. Baby Tass was so happy when we noticed he was pointing fish out to us by smacking his lips that he wanted to spend all day looking at fish. He was so excited he found it hard to stop giggling and bouncing, even at nap time, for a couple of days. Next, he wanted to broaden the topics of conversation. He would look at a picture of a squirrel, look at Brigid, look back at the squirrel, back at Brigid and then, with a questioning expression, smack his lips just once, as though to say, 'Can we talk about this animal too, using that noise?'

Psychologist Linda Acredolo noticed how keen her own daughter was to communicate in this way, months before she could 'really' talk. Her attempts to make this possible grew into the global phenomenon of baby signing.

Baby signing

Baby signing takes advantage of the fact that babies' *comprehension* of words is usually many months ahead of their ability to produce them. For your baby, learning to speak is partly a matter of waiting not only for the parts of the brain that will control vocal production, but also for their mouth and throat to develop sufficiently for them to control the language sounds they make. For this reason, it makes sense to give your baby a way to communicate with you in the meantime. Some research shows that babies who use baby signing, talk earlier and have a wider vocabulary than average, and also have higher IQ scores later on. Researchers also report that signing babies seem to have fewer tantrums, because they can communicate what they want more effectively, and have a closer bond with their carers, because they can share thoughts earlier on.

Some experts still believe that we can't yet be absolutely sure that baby signing produces better results than other kinds of close, interested engagement between babies and adults, though it is certainly plausible that it might. This may be especially true for children who will be late talkers. These children often suffer in the long term because of their early inability to communicate effectively.

Certainly, many parents find the ability of their babies to 'talk' to them with signs before they are even a year old extremely exciting, and a big motivation to keep talking and signing.

Even more persuasively, babies seem to love signing. They seem very motivated indeed to learn new signs, and overjoyed when they can make themselves understood.

There's no need to worry, though, about exactly *how* you teach your baby signs. You might like to join a baby signing class, or buy a book. But this isn't essential.

Here are the basics you need to know:

WHEN?

Some babies sign as early as six months, though eight or nine months is a more common age for a first sign. You might want to start teaching signs early in the second half of your baby's first year. Then keep it up until your baby's spoken language takes off.

WHAT?

Start with signs for things in which your baby is really interested. First signs can be either things – 'milk', 'bear', 'ball' – or activity words like 'sleep', 'love' and 'kick'. If you have a house tour set up for your baby (see Chapter 6), you might want to think of signs for the things you see. Some babies will be best at abstract words like 'hurt' or 'help', others will love words for things, especially animals. Go with the flow.

HOW?

Start with a small number of signs, and repeat them until your baby shows signs of making them themselves. Once baby is into the signing, you may be able to teach a few new signs every day. We like to start with signs that are very easy for a baby under nine months to make, without worrying about motor skills – arms flapping for 'bird', for example. Make the sign each time you say the word. Say the word very clearly and exaggeratedly, and make the sign, several times over. If baby is not looking, call them first, until they look at you, and then say, 'That's a BIRD, yes, a BIRD!', flapping your arms (wings). Try to stick with signs that are easy for your baby to make, whatever stage they are at, and which are easy for you to remember. It helps if the sign in some way mimics the thing it refers to, like the wings of a 'bird'. You can gently help your baby make the sign. Flap their arms as you say 'bird'. We also like to use animal noises, not strictly speaking signs at all, but much easier for baby to copy than true language sounds.

Word	Sign
'bird'	flap your arms, and breathe in and out through pursed lips
'pig'	snort, and put finger on nose
'food'	put finger tips to your lips
'milk'	make a fist, and open and close it, as though milking
'all gone'	move your hand, palm up, backwards and forwards
'cat'	draw your fingers across your cheek, like whiskers
'scared'	tap your chest repeatedly
'hot'	put your finger out and pull it back quickly
'where?'	shrug your shoulders, with your palms held out
'rabbit'	wrinkling up your nose, waggle two hands like ears above your head
'car'	steer an imaginary wheel while you say 'brrrrrrrr'
'cold'	hug yourself and shiver
'book'	holding hands flat with palms up
'ball'	make over-arm throwing gesture
'bear'	make your hands like claws, and move them to and fro in front of your chest as you say 'grrr'

Don't feel that you must start with obvious common words. Go with words you feel your child would most like to use. In our house, 'camel' (spitting gesture – camels do that) was a first sign, but three hundred signs later, we still hadn't learned 'milk' – probably because Ide found that grabbing the blouse and burrowing frantically worked as a perfectly good sign for that!

Your baby's first sounds

In a way, your baby is practising for talking right from birth. They need to strengthen and refine their vocal muscles, which require a lot of practice because they are constantly growing and changing. The very first non-crying sounds your baby learns will be vowel-sounds, called 'cooing'. Around six months, a few consonant sounds will creep in: baby will say 'nah', 'daa', as well as 'ah' and 'ee'. As they become more sophisticated, they will move on to two-syllable combinations, 'ee-nah', 'ah-ga'. Around seven to eight months, they will move on to what we call 'reiterative babbling', going 'gagagagaga', or 'nahnahnahnahnah'. This is considered a big milestone on the way towards speech. Next comes 'variegated babbling', where baby strings different vowel-consonant combinations together – 'degiladigabubu'.

Funnily enough, even deaf babies will start to babble at seven to eight months. But because they cannot hear, they eventually stop making these sounds. However, deaf babies with parents who communicate in sign language will 'babble' with their hands, making 'pieces' of words with their fingers. Babbling is a crucial step on the way to language.

Another amazing fact about babbling is that, although all babies around the world start off babbling at around the same age, in just the same way, within a matter of weeks babies are babbling in their native language. In other words, they use sound combinations and intonations typical of this language, and begin to lose the ability to distinguish between similar but different sounds that, in their native language, are heard as being as the same. Adults can make a good guess at the nationality of a ten-month-old from the sound of their babbling!

Recognizing first words

What counts as your baby's first word depends less on what they say than on what they mean to say. Seven- to eight-month-olds all over the world say 'mama', but few of them mean 'mother' when they say it. (Interestingly, the words for 'mother' in languages from all over the world are all very close to 'mama', which suggests that we call mothers those names because that is the first sound that babies make.) The same is true for 'dada' and 'nana'. For these sounds to count as words, they need to be used to refer to the person they belong to.

The interaction between you and your baby is what will gradually make what start off as mere sounds into the first real words. It may be no bad thing that many parents think their babies are calling their names when they are really just practising babbling. Your excited reaction whenever baby says 'mama' when you are around will encourage them to associate the sound with you, so that very soon they will mean what they say. So don't worry about giving your baby the benefit of the doubt, and assuming that they are talking to you when they might not be. It is much better to err in that direction than to fail to react when they really are calling out for you! In fact, research shows that babies whose mothers believe they are using words to refer to things will actually use words earlier than if their mothers had been more sceptical.

Remember, even the brainiest babies of this age have vocal chords that make it hard or impossible for them to pronounce most words properly and, in any case, their vocal tracts are changing so quickly that it is a real challenge to stay in control of the noises they make.

Little echo

As their babies get older, parents all over the world start not only to label things for their babies, but also to encourage their babies to echo the words they use. Some languages even have one word to express 'repeat after me'. Make a habit of this, and you may help your baby learn to speak new words.

First, make sure your baby is looking at and attending to the thing or action you are going to talk about. Then say 'CAT, it's a CAT – can you say CAT?' Exaggerate the mouth movements that go with speaking the word, and then give your baby a chance to answer (they may need quite a bit longer than you think). Sometimes your baby will respond with a completely different noise – welcome that effort too by repeating back to baby their own noise 'You said 'bub' – 'bub'! But this is a CAT – CAT!'

If your baby can repeat a word after you so that it sounds similar, it shows that they have a good mastery of their vocal instrument and is practising the crucial skill of imitating

(*Contd*)

sounds, but it doesn't show that they have really mastered the word. The magic moment comes when they echo a word they have heard you use, in a new situation to make their own point.

PROTO-WORDS AND CONTEXT-BOUND WORDS

A baby who uses their own private noise, such as 'bobobo', to comment whenever their older sister comes into the room, or who says 'nahnahnah' whenever they want their beaker, may not sound as though they are making much progress, but they are in fact taking steps towards real talking. They are using arbitrary signs for communication: a significant step in the right direction.

Another intermediate step towards real words, which some babies take, is the use of context-bound words. A baby might say something that sounds like 'car' when leaving the house, for example, especially if in the past you have often said 'Let's go out in the car!' as you open the front door. If they only say 'car' at this particular moment and in this place, they aren't quite using a real word. When they say 'car' at other times, such as when they see the picture of a racer on their new t-shirt, then they will really be using a word in the strongest sense.

For what your baby says to count as true words, their sound must sound at least a little bit like a word used by other people around them for something related to what they are talking about. They must know what they mean by a sound, always using it for the same type of thing. They must use the word to tell you about something, not just copy what you say. And they must be able to use the word in contexts in which they have not heard it used before. It doesn't matter, though, if baby means something slightly different from what you mean by a particular word. If they decide that 'dada' can refer not only to Daddy but to Granddad, Uncle Steve, and the postman as well, that's still a proper 'word'.

Keep a diary of first words. Include proto-words and context-bound words, and make a note of the way the baby uses them. You will find it easiest (and so, best) to keep the diary when your baby is just starting out, at which point you will find you need to add new words only once a month or once a week. Soon after that, baby's words will start coming too quickly for you to keep up.

The diary can be useful to help you keep friends and family who are going to spend time with baby, informed about what baby can say. If you are a maths wizard, you could even chart the number of words baby can say against their age on a graph. You will see that the line rises very gradually at first, before suddenly getting dramatically steeper and steeper as they reach the 'vocabulary explosion'.

The word-hoard grows

It will take baby quite a while to get much beyond 'Mama' and 'Dada'. These words may appear during the first year, but it may be several months before many new ones are added. Don't worry about how long the process takes. It has more to do with the physical development of your baby's vocal tract than with their mental development. There is no correlation between the number of words a baby can speak early in their second year and their vocabulary later on. Whether they can follow or produce a 'point' early on is actually a much better predictor.

At first new words will come slowly, and may sound little like words. You may think that it will take baby a very long time to get talking at this rate. Soon though, usually sometime after the middle of the second year, talking takes off. The first 30 to 50 words accumulate slowly, but after that you will find that your baby suddenly progresses to hundreds of words and sometimes even two-word sentences in a matter of weeks. This 'vocabulary explosion' is founded upon the work you've been doing in expanding the range of words your baby comprehends. Once baby's vocal muscles are ready for them to talk, and they have grasped the fact that they can be a talker too, they are ready to say all the hundreds of words they already understand. You will soon find you can't keep up with recording all the new words your child is saying. We'll talk more about this vocabulary explosion in our next chapter on language.

Listen to baby as carefully as possible, and **watch for patterns in what they say**. Some of Ide's first words were 'mu', for mushroom, and 'kkkki' for cheese. These were very definitely real words, used only for the things she meant, and used in all sorts of contexts, but they didn't sound any more word-like than the other seemingly random noises she was making at that age. It can be a real challenge to recognize the new words your baby makes. Sometimes they will excitedly name something, and you will have to struggle to connect their noises and excitement with the item they might be naming. Remember to **share the discoveries you've made about what baby can say** with other people who look after her.

Watch out for problems

There is a huge variation in the age at which babies learn to talk, and your child's number of spoken words should be very far down the list of your worries as a parent and brain trainer. Babies have individual timetables, and different paths towards fluent speech. Some children seem to wait to start talking until they are almost ready to speak in clear sentences.

A more significant measure of your child's development is the number of words they understand, but still, there is big variation here. At ten months, a good number of normal healthy babies understand only 11 words or fewer, while a similar number understand more than 150! If, by the end of the first year, your baby does not seem to understand many words, or if, by 18 months, they do not seem to understand quite a lot of what you say to them, you may need to have them checked by a doctor.

Note: You should be especially vigilant if your baby makes little eye contact, has no baby signs, babbles rarely, and does not react to quiet noises.

The most common cause of language delay is a hearing problem. Usually these are caused by something as basic as an ear infection. Between a third and a half of all babies and toddlers will get an ear infection following a cold or flu at some point, and such infections often recur persistently. They can lead to a build up of fluid in baby's ears, which may interfere with their hearing for weeks or even months at a time, just when they need to be tuning in to language.

Ear infections are quite easy to treat, but are the cause of many language delays.

To guard your baby against language delay caused by ear infections, you should:

▶ **Breastfeed if you can.** This makes ear infections far less likely and less severe.
▶ **Be alert to hearing changes.** Watch how your baby reacts to sounds like the 'bing' of the toaster in the next room, or to a whisper from you. Test your baby's alertness to low noises from time to time. If there is a drop off in their reactions, consider a check-up with the doctor.
▶ **Take your baby to the doctor for a check-up if you are concerned.** If your baby gets a really bad cold that lasts more than a week and progresses to become feverish and/or very thick and snotty, consider taking them to have their ears checked. Remember that even after your baby seems on the mend, their hearing may still be impaired. If your doctor does diagnose an ear infection, it is essential that you come back for another check-up a couple of weeks later, to make sure that your baby's ears have cleared properly.
▶ **Don't court colds and flu.** All babies catch colds from time to time, this is unavoidable, and the chances are they will not bother your baby a bit. On the other hand, it does make sense to keep babies away from people you know are sick with a cold or flu when you can. The threat to a baby's ears does make a cold a bit more of a worry for them than for you.

Analyse the first words

When your baby has 50 words, or even much earlier if you like, try looking at what kinds of words they are. Some babies, who psychologists call 'expressive', at first learn mostly words that relate to the social situation they are in: words like 'hi', 'bye', 'please', 'thank you', 'well done'. Others, called 'referential' babies, focus at first on words for things: 'cat', 'ball', 'cheese'. Babies vary hugely on this front. Some have more than twice as many words for things among their first 50 words than others. Why? These differences may tell you something about the personality of your baby. It may also reflect a little about your own. Which do you emphasize more when you talk to your baby: social or referential words? First-born children are more likely to have a lot of referential words, while second babies may have more social words, perhaps because they are often part of a busier, more social regime. First babies often have a slight edge when it comes to the size of their vocabulary, whereas second babies often show more precocious social skills.

Comprehending language is one of the most important and impressive skills your baby learns during their first years. It's easy to think of all the varieties of their other learning as stepping stones towards this one big, vital, super-sophisticated talent. But in fact language skills can actually help your baby develop what seem like more basic abilities too. The way you teach your baby to speak may affect their other non-linguistic skills in quite dramatic ways.

For example, in Korean, many sentences contain no noun. In English this is very unusual. A Korean mother, as she tidies up the toys, might say to her baby something the equivalent of 'Going in!' An English-speaking mother, on the other hand, is more likely to say things like, 'We'll put the BALL into the BOX!'

If we compare Korean- and English-speaking babies in their second year, there are some fascinating differences. English-speaking babies are much better at putting things into groups according to likeness. But Korean babies are better at figuring out how to use a rake to get an out-of-reach toy. The way English-speaking mothers teach their babies to speak gives their babies a head start in one sort of understanding of the world – the way things can be categorized – and the way Korean-speaking mothers teach language encourages another – the way actions can be put together.

Helping your baby learn language, then, turns out to be a huge factor in all of their other learning as well.

YOUR TURN

▶ Talk to your baby as much as you can.

▶ Do not be inhibited about using 'motherese' to talk to your baby. Generally, the more silly your voice sounds, the better it works to teach your baby.

▶ Label things for your baby constantly. Use pointing, clicking or tapping to attract their attention to whatever you are talking about. Name the moving things that naturally attract their gaze.

▶ Watch your baby, and try to talk to them about whatever they are looking at. Notice when they begin to point, and respond to their attempts to direct your attention.

▶ Encourage your baby to watch you talk, and to imitate noises.

▶ Consider using baby signs.

▶ Listen carefully to your baby, and be ready to spot the first words. Be willing to give them the benefit of the doubt if you aren't sure whether they are really meaning something.

▶ Keep a diary of the words your baby can say.

▶ Share the information in the diary with everyone who looks after your baby, so they can look out for and recognize new words too.

▶ Read picture books to your baby, making a point of talking around the words on the page.

▶ As well as labelling objects, stress other parts of speech such as doing-words (verbs), and prepositions such as 'in', 'on' and 'out'.

▶ Whenever your baby has a cold, look out for ear infections afterwards. Check that they still seem to hear when you whisper.

8

Training your moving, meaning, emotional baby: eight to 12 months

In this chapter you will learn:
- *to manage the growing sophistication of your baby's social impulses*
- *about brain developments that let your baby play in new ways*
- *new games that build on baby's latest skills.*

During this period, the frontal lobes of the cerebral cortex of your baby's brain, areas used for executing deliberate actions and planning ahead, are developing quickly. They have mastered enough control over their own body to sit up, move about (one way or another), and to get hold of objects, and having refined their perceptions of their environment, enough to have a good working understanding of its most basic physical properties. Now your baby is ready not only to hone their physical skills but also to make plans and to execute them. They are beginning to master the waves of unregulated and internally generated tension and distress that governed their earlier months, and are competent at making contact and bonding with the people around them. Now, as they seek to build more complex relationships, their feelings become more subtle and more obviously and complexly related to particular external events.

As a newborn, your baby was interested above all in you. Then, from three months on, they became increasingly interested in objects. Now they enter a triangular relationship with you and the things around them: they are not only interested in things, but in what you think about them, and in letting you know what they think of them or would like to do with them.

Your emotionally complicated baby

One of the most exciting things about your baby's development during this period is the way in which their emotional interactions with people become more intense and complicated. Human beings are outstanding in terms of the intricacies of their personal relationships: these, more than anything, are what make us human. From birth, your baby has shown an innate interest in people and aptitude for winning them over. But so far, they may have seemed a pretty uncomplicated sort of social being, with a smile and a chuckle for anyone ready to tickle them under the chin or make an unexpected silly noise. Sometime during the second half of the first year, however, your baby may seem quite suddenly to become a less straightforward emotional creature. They seem to react not just to unpleasant sights, sounds and feelings, but also to worries about what's going on. Watch your baby hide their face in your shoulder when something worries them, eventually peeping out apprehensively, with suspicious eyes, for another look at whatever spooked them, before they hide their eyes again. Sometimes sounds or unusual sights can trigger this reaction, but increasingly it's people. Suddenly it is clear that, from your baby's point of view, other people are not just useful for getting snacks or putting on a bit of slapstick entertainment: they are the objects of intense interpretation, obsession, devotion, and anxiety.

Separation anxiety

The most obvious of your emotionally newly complex baby's new worries will be about separation from you. Most commonly, babies who are upset by being separated from their closest, most regular care-giver, whether or not that is their mother. But we have known babies who cry when any one of their inner circle leaves the room. Babies vary greatly in the degree of their separation anxiety, with some finding even a metre or two between them and their object of adoration too much to bear. If your baby takes this view, it is going to make life a bit (or even a lot!) more difficult for a time, but feel assured that your baby's anxiety is a healthy sign of normal development, and not a symptom of bad training or 'spoiling' on your part. Babies all over the world, in all sorts of cultural environments, develop separation anxiety at this age, and its intensity is not related to the degree to which it is 'indulged' by parents. Wanting to be close to their nearest and dearest is an adaptive instinct for a baby of this age. Many experts believe that it may be a baby's way of ensuring they stay close to an experienced brain trainer who understands where they are at and who can help them learn effectively. **You cannot 'train' your baby out of their separation anxiety, so don't try.**

Insight: separation anxiety comes in waves

Around six months, Tass would become distraught whenever I left his side. At the moment, at eleven months, he's unworried about separation from me as long as there is someone else he trusts nearby. This is typical. It's likely that his anxiety will come and go for years to come.

If you did succeed in eliminating your baby's protests at your departures, you would probably not have helped their developing inner world. Some toddlers, who psychologists describe as 'insecurely attached', try to appear indifferent when left by their mothers. But on the inside these babies are still stressed by the separation, and will later run a higher risk of psychological problems than babies who have not been forced to develop a 'stiff upper lip' at such a tender age. **Do all you can to accommodate your baby's worries about separation from you.**

Some babies mainly become anxious if they actually see a beloved one leaving the room, or hear their voice when they can't see them. If you just need to fetch something from the next room, get used to sneaking in and out. If someone else is taking care of your baby while you get other things done nearby, get used to keeping quiet so that your baby can bond with that other individual, without being reminded of you.

Babies are often more worried about separation when they are tired, hungry or sick. Keep a note of your baby's current level of anxiety, and **avoid scheduling one-off separations, or new routines such as nursery, for stages or times when your baby is particularly anxious.**

Reading faces

Apart from the fact that your baby knows you are likely to be their best brain trainer, they have another good reason to want to stay close to their nearest and dearest. By this age, they are learning more and more every day from watching your face. Even as a newborn they were able to differentiate between expressions suggesting different emotions, and to copy such expressions, and instinctively respond to your smile and the joy on your face. But now your baby's approach becomes more analytic. You may catch your baby looking narrowly into your face, as though to read it. That is just what they are trying to do. Towards the end of the first year we see big developments in what we call 'social referencing': the way your baby reads your face and behaviour to help them decide what to make of a particular situation.

This becomes more obvious as your baby gets mobile. Try introducing a new (and ever so slightly alarming) toy at the other side of the room. Researchers have used a toy dog that barks intermittently. As your baby crawls off to have a closer look, do they look back at you to see what you make of the situation? Try looking concerned and as if you are about to jump from your seat to intervene. Does your baby stop in their tracks? Some research has shown that girl babies have a lower threshold for picking up concern than boy babies, so that the parents of boys tend to use more exaggerated negative facial expressions to discourage their babies from dangerous exploration.

Insight: gauge your individual baby's sensitivity

Tass just headed towards the open door at the top of the stairs. I yelped and flung the laptop off my lap. Tass stopped, his face crumpled, and he dissolved into distraught tears! He will check my reaction before heading that way again, but I must try not to terrify him too often.

In watching your face, baby is learning a social skill they will use all their life, and which will be of great use to you much sooner. A baby who 'checks' with you before trying a new thing, and who is responsive to your reactions, is much easier to keep safe than one who does not. Make sure you spend time watching your baby play, ready to encourage or discourage them as they look back at you. As babies get older, research shows that they give up trying to check adult reactions if the adult present never seems to look at the thing they are looking at.

Make sure that you match words with reactions. Say, 'No, no, no!' as you spring from your chair to stop them licking the soles of your outdoor shoes, and avoid giving too many weary, unconcerned 'Don't do that's', while you sit still on the sofa. This will confuse your baby about the meaning of your words. They are already keen to follow your instructions and judgement, and that, for both your sakes, is definitely a skill to be cultivated.

Stranger anxiety

Another sign of the growing subtlety of your baby's emotional responses may show up in their reaction to strangers, or even to acquaintances beyond their most intimate circle. At five months, most babies will beam over your shoulder at the grumpiest fellow bus passenger, and giggle at the postman even if he has the most formidable beard. But sometime later, many babies start to be shy of people they don't know, and some may become positively terrified. This may happen before the end of the first year, or not until a bit later. Many babies are more frightened of strange men than of women, and some find hats, facial hair or dark glasses particularly spooky. Ide was terrified even of granddad Fergus when he had his glasses on, and she would shake with fear if she saw even a picture of a person wearing glasses.

The common fear of glasses and beards gives us a clue to some of the psychological developments behind stranger anxiety. As we discussed above, during this period babies are working hard on reading faces, and are building their skill at learning about situations as well as about other people from the emotional reactions registered on faces. People we don't know are harder to 'read' in this way than those we know better, and dark glasses and beards can seriously obstruct the view!

Your baby's sudden fear of their grandparents from out of town may be very embarrassing and inconvenient, but patience with your baby's feeling is essential. Your baby will get used to less familiar people if they get to encounter them regularly on their own terms.

You may be able to reassure your baby somewhat by relaxing yourself and showing your trust of the stranger through your own body language. On the other hand, **taking your baby up too close, or forcing them into physical contact with the person they are anxious about will make matters worse.** You may also find that your baby is more worried about strangers in small, intimate spaces than they are in the middle of a public space with other people around. They may particularly dislike entering unfamiliar houses or having strangers come into their own territory.

If it is particularly important that your baby should react positively to a particular person, **set up the meeting carefully**. Make sure your baby is not tired or hungry, and that they are safe in the arms of a favourite care-giver when the new person turns up. Talk to them about what is about to happen, and prepare them for something unusual. If possible, arrange for their first meeting to be on neutral but familiar territory – in a supermarket, for instance. It is much easier to try to avoid your baby freaking out about a new person in the first place, than it is to reassure them about them once they are already spooked.

Strange things

During this period you may also notice that your baby becomes more wary of new things, as well as of new people. Psychologists believe that, again, this anxiety may be the symptom of their developing intelligence and understanding of the world. By this age, babies can recall previous experiences more effectively than when they were younger. A developing memory, along with other developments in the prefrontal cortex, make it easier for babies to respond not only to the superficial look of objects around them, but also to try to analyse and make deeper sense of familiar things. Your baby may, for example, feel they know quite a bit about balls: they are spherical things that people roll and throw to them, balls are safe to touch, unlikely to bring a 'No, no, no!' from mother, and baby doesn't expect them to talk, to be very hot or cold, or to move by themselves. When your baby encounters an obviously familiar *type* of thing, they feel they can make a range of predictions about it, and about what it is appropriate for them to do with it. On the other hand, if you introduce a wholly new kind of thing, or a familiar thing that looks in some way significantly unusual, your baby may be disconcerted by the fact that they do not know what to expect of this particular thing. They may be very wary in exploring it, and keep checking your face for encouragement and reassurance.

You can reassure them, as well as help build both their understanding of things and their vocabulary, by demonstrating how the new object works. If it opens, show them how, reminding them of more familiar boxes by saying, 'Open – closed!' or whatever, in your usual way. Point out familiar images on the new thing, or name the colours on it. Bang it with something to show them how it makes a familiar plastic/wood/metal noise, or let them feel the familiar cloth texture on their cheek. Talk it all through as you demonstrate.

Advancing play moves

In the previous phase of development, your baby's play mainly involved manipulating single objects: passing them from hand to hand, and then from hand to mouth, maybe putting them down and picking them back up. Now, during this next period, that sort of manipulation carries on, but babies also become fascinated by what they can do with two objects together. They start to bang and scratch one thing against another, to drop things through holes, put one thing inside another, and, eventually, to build things one on top of the other. Towards the end of this period your baby may be ready to use toys like stacking rings, cups and shape puzzles 'properly'. In the meantime encourage them to play in a wide range of ways with the random objects they have been fond of during the earlier months.

SHOW THEM HOW TO PUT ONE THING INTO ANOTHER

Compare their reaction when you put a ball inside an opaque plastic cup to when you put it inside something see-through. Show them the different noises things make when you put them inside one another and shake. Your baby will enjoy different sorts of boxes with lids they can open and close, hiding and revealing the things inside by turns. You could try some supervised play with a jack-in-the-box, or a music box that activates a dancing ballerina.

ATTACH ONE THING TO ANOTHER

Show baby how to pull something towards them by tugging on a string attached to the object. Push short bits of ribbon through the holes or loops in familiar toys. Squeeze a rubber ring around a favourite ball. Show them how you attach the links of a plastic chain together.

DROP ONE THING THROUGH ANOTHER

Your baby may still lack the dexterity to fit shapes through the right holes in a shape-sorter, but they will soon get the hang of dropping random small items through an empty kitchen roll tube. Look out for interesting holes or crevices in the backs of chairs and other furniture that baby can post things through.

OTHER IDEAS TO ADVANCE PLAY MOVES

Demonstrate the different noises you can make banging or scraping one thing against another.

Bring out the blocks, and begin modelling tower building. Build other random objects on top of one another.

Small is beautiful

Be careful: Notice how your baby now immediately spots any small item on the carpet – a sequin, a crumb, a piece of fluff – and aims to get it into their mouth as quickly as possible. They become fascinated by all things small near the start of this period, just when they are able to pick them up. At first they will do so clumsily, using the side of their thumb and forefinger. But gradually their pick-ups get more precise, until they are using just the very tips of thumb and forefinger like pincers. This is an important motor skill and will feed a new, more detailed, view of the world.

There is a real tension, particularly at the start of this period, between baby's obsessive interest in small things and their enthusiasm for putting everything in their mouth. This may begin to wane towards the end of the year, especially if you consistently discourage them from mouthing small things that are not food. In the meantime you need to make sure they have plenty of safe small things to pick up. Try edible flower petals, rosemary leaves or other bits of herbs, defrosted peas, and small soft berries.

HIDE AND SEEK

For a long time, psychologists have believed that babies develop 'object permanence' (that is, the understanding that things continue to exist even when they are out of sight) during this period of their developments. While recent research questions this, it is certainly true that babies show growing interest in things that are out of sight. Unsurprisingly, mobile babies seem to have a better understanding of the fact that an out-of-sight object is still there, available to be fetched out, than babies of the same age who are not yet moving.

As soon as your baby can get around on their own, get one of their soft toys to scuttle off, while baby watches, and hide it behind the sofa leg. Your baby should set off to find their toy. If, half way, they seem to forget where they are going, get the toy to peep out to remind them. Most babies love this game. It exercises their ability to focus on something out of sight, gives practice with forming a plan and sticking with it for some time, and also involves a bit of simple but concrete pretend play, as you get the toy to walk, hide and peep. Pretend play will be one of the next skills that baby will work on.

GAMES WITH RULES

As your baby's memory, ability to think ahead, and desire and ambition for control over their environment grows, you will see the growth of a play style that will persist throughout much of childhood. Your baby will start to make up games with rules and patterns. The rules will make no sense to you, seeming completely arbitrary, but babies seem to practise the skills they will need later on to play 'real' games or to learn useful patterns of activity, by setting and internalizing their own sets of rules.

Insight: crazy games
Nine-month-old Tass picks up a lunchbox and walks down the hall to a certain point, and then walks back. He puts down the lunchbox and picks up a bottle, walks down the hall again to the same point, comes back, and picks up the lunchbox again. He spends ages doing these 'shuttle runs'.

Your baby will be particularly delighted if they can rope you in to their games. Following their own rules *and* getting someone else to follow them is the ultimate achievement. Tass holds his favourite ball and tugs on his grandmother Pat's legs to be picked up. She picks him up into her lap and he drops the ball. He squirms to be put down, and crawls off to fetch the ball, then wants to come up again. He drops the ball once more, and so it goes on.

This sort of coordinated, patterned physical and mental activity is a real sign of your baby's growing sophistication. This is the sort of pure play that childhood is all about. Human children spend a lot of time in activities with absolutely no immediate useful object, but which, by their exceptional complexity and originality, provide the foundation for intelligent, innovative and adaptable adult behaviour.

YOUR TURN

▶ Make sure you keep up lots of face-to-face contact and conversation with your baby.

▶ Be ready to reassure your baby when they start to show a new range of more complicated anxieties relating to new people, situations and objects. They are actually being clever and adaptive, not silly.

▶ Indulge your baby's growing need to be close to you whenever you can without fear of 'spoiling'.

▶ Build on your baby's increasing sensitivity to your psychological attitude. Use calm and reassuring words and gestures to calm them, and a joyful expression to encourage their play.

▶ Use words as well as physical intervention to control your baby: a careful warning voice and manner will do much to guard them from danger and mischief.

▶ Be ready to join your baby in the repetitive games that they may try to initiate.

▶ Make an effort to find playthings that match the skills your baby is working on. The right objects will delight them and give you a break while they really get to work.

▶ Provide safe, small objects so that your baby can practise fine motor skills.

▶ Demonstrate advanced play manoeuvres involving more than one object: model putting one thing in another, one thing through another, one thing on top of another, hitting, banging or pushing one thing with another, and so on.

9

Brain training for toddlers: 12 to 24 months

In this chapter you will learn:
- *how your toddler learns through imaginative and imitative play*
- *about your toddler's new abilities to plan and think ahead*
- *about the new insights your toddler is developing into other people.*

This is an exciting period, during which most babies get really confident about getting around, and then begin to master language. The new skills your baby is learning may seem so numerous and so complex that it is hard to keep up with them. Physical dexterity opens up many new play opportunities, as does a new, more complicated understanding of the world, which comprehends not only the way things are but the way things might be. Your baby's social interactions are now extremely complex, involving shared plans, games and fantasies.

Copycat

Your baby now knows how to use things like utensils, hair-brushes, and a cloth for wiping. They begin the imitative play that will continue for many years. Your baby will tend to enjoy imitating the actions which those around them perform most often: this play is an important step towards independence. Babies learn very quickly and have impressive memories. In one experiment, 18-month-olds watched an experimenter touch his forehead to a box to make it light up. A week later babies were given the same box to play with. They remembered the demonstration, and touched it to their foreheads to make it light up! So you can see that it is important that your baby spends lots of time where they can see what you're doing. Let them sit in the highchair within reach when you cook sometimes, or bring them along with you while you do household chores.

Insight

Ide has a toy ironing board and oven, but she has hardly ever played with them. However, she has a drawer filled with 'paper work', and spends many hours 'filling in forms' and 'working' on a burnt-out laptop. Brigid fears she is not modelling the role of domestic goddess too well...

Baby orangutans spend all day being carried by their mother. During infancy they learn, from scratch, how to recognize and consume the hundreds of different plants available to eat in their particular habitat. Human babies learn in the same way, but because our brains are bigger and our activity so much more varied, they have far more to learn. Your baby will love watching you do practical tasks, toddling right into the middle of the action to 'help' you construct that piece of flat pack furniture. Don't underestimate how much they learn in this way. Indeed, it's likely that you will be amazed to see that tasks they only witnessed once crop up as important features in their pretend play.

Pretend play

Another big landmark that your baby will arrive at early in this period is the ability to pretend that one thing is another. To start with, they may pretend that an empty toilet roll is a car or a phone. Next, they will use two objects to pretend with at the same time: perhaps they'll 'cook' the toilet roll in a baseball cap. They may also start to pretend that inanimate toys are animate, getting their doll to cry, or their dog to bark or to steal your food.

This pretend play reveals a lot about the amazing developments in your baby's brain. The ability to understand one thing as 'standing' for another is a very important, distinctively human capacity, which is crucial to both language and mathematics. It is also crucial to all sorts of imaginative creativity.

Imaginative play will be central to your child's world for years to come, and has other important implications for the development of their intelligence. When your child imagines, they are using a mental model of how the world might be: if that piece of log were a cup of tea, you would hold it the right way up; if it tipped over, you could mop up the mess with a cloth and you might wag your finger at the person who spilled it for being careless. In order to make up a coherent make-believe world, your child has to put together information about causes and effects and the way events and actions are usually linked together in the real world.

This grasp of cause and effect, and the ability it gives us to learn from what happened, predict what *will* happen and imagine what *could* happen, are crucial to human intelligence – to all the arts and all the sciences. It's this ability that allows us to change our world for the better. You can watch your child's grasp of cause and effect mature during the second year.

A while after their first birthday, watch how they solve a practical problem like how to reach a high drawer or a toy that has rolled under the sofa. At this stage, they will use mainly trial and error to solve these problems, as animals do. You have probably noticed that one-year-olds are incredibly energetic and systematic in their experiments to find out what happens if you randomly combine different objects and actions (*that's* why you found porridge poked into the keyhole). They can often figure tricky things out this way. Give them a rake to reach a toy that's rolled out of reach, and they will randomly try various ways of using it to get what they want. In the course of their efforts, they learn more and more about cause and effect.

With all that energetic experimentation under their belt, six months later your baby is much more likely to use planning skills, rather than just trial and error, in these sorts of situations. Just by looking at the rake, they can see just how it could be used to help reach their toy. If there is a box on the floor near their high drawer, they will automatically imagine how it might be used as a step to help them reach. Before they can speak, human babies are already moving towards a type of forward planning and causal understanding that are uniquely human.

Can you do anything to encourage this exciting development? You probably just need to give your child time, space, opportunity and encouragement to experiment with their world.

Don't fill their schedule with structured activities, no matter how 'educational', if it leaves little time in their day for what looks to adult eyes like aimless 'messing about'. This messing about is how babies learn. **Don't try to get them to play with toys only in the way they are designed to be played with.** If they want to use bricks rather than their toy tea set for a tea party, let them. If they want to spend ages trying how many parts of their tea set will fit inside their rubber boot, fine. The random, trial-and-error experiments will feed a causal map of the world, which can be the basis for ingenious practical solutions as well as elaborate and absorbing fantasies.

Experimenting on you

In the same way as your baby conducts experiments to figure out how things in the world work and interact, they also set about exploring how *people* work. As your baby approaches their second birthday and the 'terrible twos', you may notice 'testing' behaviour. They will approach the forbidden shelf of glass jars while watching your face for a horrified reaction. It seems like they want to break rules just to upset you.

But upsetting you isn't their goal. They are exploring the fascinating fact that they want one thing and you want something different. They are exploring your reactions, checking them for consistency and predictability.

You can **help your baby form a coherent and positive model of the way people work by being consistent and loving in your own responses.** Make sure they take away from their interactions with you the lesson you would like to give them about human nature.

Between one and two years old, based on their developing understanding of the feelings of other people, your baby will also begin to show kindness. From birth, babies find the sound of other babies' distress stressful and upsetting, just as adults do. But, when they are younger, they will try to feel better by looking for a cuddle for themselves, rather than by setting out to help the distressed baby. Later on, though, they may offer a toy to cheer up a crying friend. As they become more sophisticated, they may offer the friend's favourite toy, instead of assuming they would be cheered by their own personal favourite.

If you try this test a while after your child's first birthday, maybe when they are 14 months old, and then again when they are one-and-a-half or older, you will see that they are learning not only about things but also about people during this period. At mealtime, present your baby with two foods, one that they like and one that they hate. Try to convince them that your own preference is the opposite of theirs. 'I love those peas – so tasty! I don't like the raisins though, too sweet, yuck…' Wait a minute, then say to them, 'Yum, I'm hungry, can I have some of your food?' Younger babies will probably offer you the food that they themselves prefer. They think that because they themselves prefer raisins to peas, everyone else must do too, so they will kindly offer you raisins. Sometime after they turn one-and-a-half, though, baby will show that they understand that different people have different preferences. They will give you the food you told them you preferred.

This experiment shows the amazing progress your baby is making. Human intelligence is uniquely adapted to understanding other people; so much so that many of our ancestors attributed human-type consciousness to the natural world itself. Note, though, how long it has taken your baby to arrive at a fairly basic understanding of the preferences of other people, and bear this in mind the next time someone absurdly suggests that they are 'manipulating you', or being 'selfish'. Other people are complicated and babies are not born understanding them. But with lots of interaction they can learn.

Discipline

There is no doubt that, as your baby gets older, you having a strong influence over the way they behave is crucial not only to the development of their intelligence but also to their safety. When your baby is young, things are straightforward: if they pick up something dangerous, we take it from them; if they kick and scream in protest, we don't blame them and don't take it personally, because they are too young to understand about rules. They don't blame us, either. As baby gets older, though, and can understand instructions, we expect them to start to do what we ask some of the time, and even to follow rules. Actually, babies often enjoy doing this. They like to show that they understand and can follow through on an instruction. Even before they are one, babies start to follow rules. For instance, if you have consistently shown disgust and alarm when they try to eat their outdoor shoes, and have consistently taken them from them when they try, they will eventually stop trying to do so. While they are learning to follow the rule, watch them as they watch you while they raise the shoes to their lips. It may look as though they are being sneaky – seeing if you are watching – but really they are checking your reaction, and testing the rule: 'Is it always bad to eat those yummy shoes?'

But what about those occasions when baby really wants to do something and we really don't want them to? How can we train them to accept that they must do what they are told without a fuss?

Unfortunately – and, of course, fortunately – human babies are not lab rats, and can't be 'trained' in the way rats can be. Because they are immature, babies are in some ways much less in control of their behaviour than rats are. If a baby is very frightened, disappointed, excited, and hungry or tired, they will literally lose control of themselves. The most consistent regime of punishments and rewards cannot stop them from, for example, clinging and crying to a departing parent, or falling apart when it turns out that the ice-cream van is closed. As they get older, their cerebral cortex will command greater control over their emotions, and they will become more reasonable in these situations. But until then, your job is to help them deal with their emotions, not to 'train' them out of your baby.

Fortunately human babies, as well as being less mature than rats, are also a whole lot cleverer than they are, especially when it comes to social relationships. For this reason, there are lots of ways that we can influence the behaviour of babies without resorting to electric shocks and bribes of food. Our relationship with our babies is not like that of a scientist to a lab rat. We love our babies, we hope and

fear for them, get exhausted and even, as they get older, annoyed by
them; the way we interact with them is shaped through and through
by emotion. For that reason, we should think of our attempts to help
our babies behave well not as a regime that is imposed upon them
by us, but rather as part of the relationship between us. The stronger
that relationship in general, the better the chance that our children
will grow up to behave well.

Because influencing your child's behaviour is part of a relationship,
it is very personal and complicated matter which cannot be boiled
down into a list of rules. But here are ten plus one top tips:

1. **Your child wants your approval.** Children learn to behave safely
   and acceptably chiefly through this powerful desire. The stronger
   the relationship between you, the more eager your child will
   be to please you. Always remember that this is your strongest
   support. Make the most of it by talking with your child about
   behaviour that is nice and behaviour that isn't, at times when
   they are actually behaving well. Make sure you notice their good
   behaviour and reward it with joy and praise.
2. **Your child learns from your example.** Unfortunately for us, we
   parents have to try to set a good one, by not shouting, hitting,
   being rude or selfish, eating crackers before meals, and all the
   hard-to-live-up-to rest of it. Children often pick up unwelcome
   behaviour from other children, especially in group situations like
   nursery. If your child must spend time with bad role-models, you
   can try to pre-empt their influence by explaining that you don't
   like biting, for example, before your child picks up the habit.
3. **Avoid the occasions for naughtiness.** Most adults wouldn't much
   like the amount of bossing and restriction that most toddlers
   have to put up with, so do your best to make life easier. The
   oftener you issue commands and say 'no', the less force your
   instructions will have. Try to set up the house so that you don't
   have to warn your baby not to touch too often. Remember
   that, no matter how firm and consistent you are, they can't help
   behaving badly when they are bored, tired, hungry or over-
   stimulated. Do all you can to keep them out of these states, and
   remember that it's not really their fault if they have a meltdown
   at 5.30 p.m. in the supermarket queue at the end of a long day.
4. **Using distraction is a key, not a cop-out.** For the first few years
   of your baby's life, you would be mad to confront each clash

of will head-on. If you can distract your baby with some sort of diversion, do.

5 **Pick your battles.** Too many commands are not good for your baby's brain development. Try not to oppose your baby's will for the sake of it, or for trivial inessential reasons. They must wear a coat to go out in the snow, but why shouldn't they wear pyjamas underneath if they really want to? Be as flexible and open-minded as you can.

6 **Treat 'attention seeking' seriously – and sympathetically.** Attention seeking is one of the most common causes of 'bad' behaviour in young children. But attention seeking isn't the sin it's often made out to be. The younger they are, the more babies rely on adult attention to grow and learn as they should. Busy modern lifestyles make this a great source of family tension because often we just don't have the time to give them the attention our children need. The odd tantrum when a toddler wants to play, but dad needs to vacuum the spare room before grandma arrives, is horrible for everyone, but is no big deal. Consistent 'bad' behaviour, on the other hand – a situation where you and your baby are upset and cross for big chunks of every day – is often a sign that you need to find more time for them. Make sure you pay attention to them when they are being good as well as, or more than, when they are playing up, otherwise the incentive is towards being naughty.

7 **Being consistent is vital.** Your child won't learn about rules that only operate some of the time. The older they get, the better they will be at internalizing rules, and the more upsetting they will find it when they aren't applied consistently. Before you tell them not to do something, or let them do something, think about whether you will be able to stick with the rule, or qualify it in a way that they will understand.

8 **Punishment doesn't work very well.** The research shows this. It is not very effective at altering particular bad behaviours, and any success on one front may be outweighed by damage to your relationship, which will lead to bad behaviour on other fronts. Smacking is a particularly ineffective and counter-productive punishment, which no sensible parent would resort to if they had read the research.

9 **All children are naughty sometimes.** Don't feel that occasional fiery confrontations are a sign either that you are not giving enough love and attention, or not being firm enough.

Throughout childhood, occasionally your child will really want something they really can't have, or impulsively do something they really shouldn't. Adults misbehave and argue with each other too. Social relationships are about conflict as well as affection, so don't blame yourself or your baby if it's not always sweetness and light.

10 **Find ways of teaching about undesirable behaviour that do not damage baby's self-esteem.** The best time to point out what is a nice way to behave and what isn't, is when your child is being good. When they are doing something naughty, try to remind them that that isn't a nice way to behave without suggesting that they, themselves are naughty. Remember that your baby's sense of self is still developing and is vulnerable to negative messages from you. If they come to believe they are naughty, or not much good, they will behave badly and feel it doesn't matter or that they can't succeed in improving their behaviour.

11 **Use words, but not words alone.** Tell your toddler kindly, specifically and clearly what it is they are doing wrong, and if possible give a reason. Instead of saying, 'Stop it!' or 'Don't be naughty!' say, 'Please don't put your hand near the pram wheels when it's moving – you could hurt yourself!' Reinforce your words with actions. If possible, get down to their level, look into their face and capture their attention before you begin. Adjust the firmness and seriousness of your tone to the importance of the lesson. For instance, 'Don't run into the road' needs your most serious voice, whereas 'Don't call Aunty Jill's dog ugly' needs a less serious one. Maybe put their hand gently into the pram wheel and show them how it could get squashed when the wheel moves.

Think of discipline as one of the ways in which you help your baby learn about the world, and not as an exercise in taming their rebellious spirit. If they feel you are on their side, you will be able to guide them and work with them until they are old enough to make sensible judgements and control their impulses themselves.

Insight: when it comes to discipline, less is more

We overheard a professional nanny recently: 'Keep off the grass! Put down those stones! Stop spinning! Put your scarf on!' She sounded really in charge! But there was her toddler, still spinning on the grass, stones in hand, with no scarf on. Would he have listened if she warned him not to run into the road?

Cuddle time

Soon your baby will be walking and running around, straying further from your side and spending less time in your arms. They may also start breastfeeding less often. These big changes mean that, almost inevitably, the physical bond between you will weaken a little, but you should do all you can to maintain contact, and never think of physical distancing as a sign of maturity that you should be pushing for. Your baby's brain still relies on closeness to a loving adult body to regain its equilibrium when things go wrong or get too exciting. Your baby will be happier, think better, and be easier to control if you can keep giving them the doses of calming, happy hormones that cuddles trigger. In some ways, cuddling is more important now than ever.

Build cuddle time into your routine. Cuddles are not just for when things go wrong. If baby is going to move to their own bed, make sure there are still cuddles before sleep. Cuddles before naps will also make them sleep more relaxed and refreshing, and once your baby cuts down or cuts out their naps altogether, breaking up the day with a couple of cuddle sessions will give you both a relaxing, reviving brain-boost that may help avoid exhaustion and tantrums.

Picture books and baby brains

At this age, picture books become a wonderful way of entertaining your baby and expanding their vocabulary. There are so many exciting things we can show a baby in a book that never or hardly ever crop up in real life: most animals, many vehicles, volcanoes, fairies, ice-cream sundaes. But have you ever stopped to think about what is involved when your child uses pictures to help them learn a word?

First of all, they associate the flat picture with a three-dimensional thing in real life. Babies can do this at five months, as they show by being less interested in a doll they have already examined in a picture, than in a new doll they have never even seen 'on paper'. As baby learns words or signs, they will be able to name pictures of things as easily as the things themselves. There is some evidence that even children raised in cultures without pictures are still able to do this at age one-and-a-half. But, at that age, children can still sometimes be a bit weird about pictures. There is a picture of a bar of chocolate in one of our books that we can't show Tass, because he will try to eat it. Ide used to try to pick up the redcurrants in the pattern on our tablecloth. Mostly babies act as though pictures are not the same as objects, but sometimes they seem to think they might be similar.

By the time they are one-and-a-half, babies have a more sophisticated understanding of pictures. About to hit the vocabulary explosion, and getting into imaginary play, they are growingly confident in their grasp of the idea that words, things, and pictures can all represent other things. Psychologists showed 18-month-olds a picture of an unfamiliar object – a whisk – and named it for them. Then, later, they presented the babies with both a real whisk and the very same picture of a whisk, and asked them to find 'the whisk'. The babies almost always handed them the real object rather than the picture. So babies are firmly onto of the idea of pictures as representations.

Picture perfect

You can test your baby's understanding of pictures yourself. Next time you buy something novel that comes packaged with an image of the product on the outside, show the image to your baby, telling them what the new thing is called a few times. Later, put both the image and the product itself in front of baby among some other familiar objects, and ask them to 'give me the Frisbee' (or whatever). Do they choose the image or the real thing? Does this change as they get older?

By two-and-a-half, babies are even more adept in their processing of pictures. Give them a simple picture or map of a room, which shows them where a toy is hidden, and they will be able to find the toy.

Top brain-training activities

PLAY 'FETCH'

You might think this is a game for dogs, but by the time they reach their second birthday, babies have developed fetching talents that far surpass Fido's. As soon as baby is mobile, start asking them to fetch you things you think they might know the name of. At first they may mostly ignore you, but they will still be learning about requests and commands, about please and thank you, and maybe about pointing, as well as getting in extra vocabulary training. Soon they will start to follow your requests, thrilled at the combination of exercise and mastery of language that the game involves. This can be a great way of finding out how many words your baby really understands: Can they fetch you the camel? What about the iPhone? As they get older, you can try more complicated instructions: 'Can you fetch me the baby wipes from the basket, please?' 'Can you fetch me the ball please – it's under the sofa,' 'Can you please go to into the hall and fetch the torch from the cupboard?' By the time they approach two, you can try even harder missions: 'Can you put the box next to the desk, so that you can stand on it and get the tissues for me, please?'

BABY'S OWN PICTURES

Most babies can scribble with a crayon by the time they turn one (though watch out, they can equally easily eat up a crayon for elevenses while your back is turned!). At first, drawing will be a purely mechanical activity that has an interesting effect, similar to waving a rattle to hear the sound. Soon, though, your baby will start to try to control the marks they make, and not too long after, to get the idea that their drawing represents something. Toward their second birthday, ask them, 'What have you drawn?' and, if they have a few words, they may tell you it's the dog. Or they may surprise you by spontaneously announcing, unprompted, that their blotch of paint is an elephant. Babies eventually come to believe that pictures represent whatever the person who drew them meant them to be, whether or not they bear any resemblance to the thing they are supposed to be. Being able to name their drawing is another example of your baby's growing understanding of how people and symbols work.

PUT-TOGETHER TOYS

Your baby's advancing grasp of forward planning and imitation, and their persistent interest in experimenting with how things interact with each other, make simple construction toys a hit during this period. Starting with stacking cups, graduated ring toys and bricks, watch how baby shifts from using trial and error to a more sophisticated understanding of size and shape to build the cups into a tower, get the rings onto the post in the right order, and build a stable tower of several bricks. Work with them to show how it's done. Make lots of encouraging noises. Shape-sorters are another great toy for the move from trial-and-error activity towards planning behaviour. Watch how your baby moves from randomly trying the shapes anywhere, to looking for the hole that actually matches the shape. When they can do this, they are ready for simple board puzzles, and then for jigsaws. Some children love stringing large beads onto shoelaces. All these games coach fine motor-skills and spatial awareness and reasoning, as well as core skills in forward planning and causal analysis of the physical world. Puzzles and stacking cups with recognizable images on them add another dimension to the game by building vocabulary too. Get used to the way your baby likes to play with you by their side, then on their own for a while, and then with more help from you again. Sensitive adjustment of input from you will help them develop their independent play.

YOUR TURN

▶ Give your baby plenty of opportunity to watch you and other people engaged in a variety of interesting activities. Talk to them about what's going on.

▶ Look out for, encourage, and join in pretend play.

▶ Allow plenty of time for experimental play, encouraging your baby to combine objects, toys, and pretending, in whatever way they like.

▶ Take extra care to behave lovingly, consistently and predictably, to help your child form a positive model of how other people work.

▶ Gradually begin to teach your toddler the rules that govern their life.

▶ Be positive but consistent in enforcing these rules, summoning all your patience to help your baby on their first steps on the long road towards controlling their own impulses.

▶ Make a conscious effort to maintain the physical connection between yourself and your toddler, with lots of cuddles.

▶ Read picture books together often, talking about the pictures as well as reading the words on the page.

▶ Introduce your baby to drawing, painting and modelling.

▶ Trawl second-hand stores for construction games and puzzles that suit your baby's stage of development.

10

....

Language: advanced manoeuvres

In this chapter you will learn:
- *how, why and when your baby's vocabulary will explode (!)*
- *how your baby moves from single words to grammatical sentences*
- *how to talk to your baby to expand their language skills.*

Your baby has already done a huge amount of heavy ground work laying the foundations for language. Now they will shock you with the speed at which they set about constructing the towering mental achievement of fluent speech.

Starting just before their first birthday, your baby slowly and painstakingly learns their first few dozen words, maybe only a few a month. Then, suddenly, the pace changes dramatically. You can expect this step-change to occur after your baby has acquired somewhere between 30 and 50 words. From now on, the average baby starts to learn about nine new words a day.

Signs of progress

Around the time of the vocabulary explosion, you may notice other changes in the way your baby uses language. They may seem, on the face of it, to get *worse* at language use on some fronts. In particular, they may be more likely than ever to call all men, 'daddy', or everything roundish, 'ball', even if they have been using these words correctly for some time. This is called 'overextension', and is very common with children beginning to talk, and we should be careful not to dismiss it lightly as a mistake. At the moment, Tass, who has been saying 'baah' just for balls and marbles for a few weeks, suddenly also says 'baah' for the moon, a rounded beaker, clocks with domed faces, traffic lights, most fruit, scoops of ice cream – you name it. A friend's baby, Eliza, has moved from calling her big brother 'Jo', to calling all his toys, his clothes, and his bedroom 'Jo', too. Why are these babies suddenly 'getting it wrong'?

Well, are they? Shakespeare can tell us the crescent moon looks 'like a silver bow new drawn in heaven', but Tass, looking at the full moon, doesn't yet have the verbal dexterity to say, 'Mum, that reminds me of a ball'. Some of your baby's overextensions may be the symptom of a poetic aptitude for analogy and comparison, and seeing the likeness between one thing and another is a keystone of intelligence.

When Eliza calls everything belonging to Jo 'Jo', she may just be doing her best to say 'That reminds me of Jo – that's Jo's'. It may also be that Tass and Eliza are just desperate to extend the conversation. They want to chat about the moon and about Jo's spelling books but haven't yet learned the words to do so.

Experiments show that babies overgeneralize much less in comprehension than in expression. Babies who call all animals 'dog' could nevertheless pick out a dog from among pictures of other animals perfectly well. So it's much more important to encourage these attempts at communication, than to worry about inaccurate word use. The most helpful response combines the signs of delighted comprehension with a bit of vocabulary extension: 'Yes!!!! It is a man like Dada! It's Uncle Steve - Uncle Steve!'

Be ready to stoke the vocabulary explosion! Your baby may start pointing to things expecting you to name them, bringing them to you for a comment, or asking 'Wozzat?' constantly. Around the time of the vocabulary spurt, babies get much better at recognizing when you are naming an object for them, and which object it is you are talking about. Just make sure you are doing the labelling they are interested in. You will notice that your baby can sometimes remember a word after being told it only once or twice, though remember that they may still need to be taught the word in infant-directed motherese.

Try these two tests of the strategies your baby uses to learn new words, before and after they reach the vocabulary spurt: First, let baby play with three things you know they know the name of, and one thing they do not know the name of. For example, baby Tass would know the names of a toy car, a cup, and a bear, but has never come across a cassette tape.

Now ask your baby, 'Give me the cassette', or you can call the unfamiliar object by a made-up name (psychologists like the word 'dax') if its real name is ambiguous or over-long.

Before the vocabulary spurt, your baby may be puzzled by this request, maybe passing you one of the other objects. But after the spurt has begun, they will immediately figure out that the 'cassette' must be the object they don't know the name of. (When we tried this with Tass he kept giving us the car no matter what we asked for, because he loves cars. Learn from our mistake, and avoid using any of your baby's favourite objects).

Next, put two unfamiliar objects a couple of feet apart on the table, in front of your baby, but beyond their reach. Sit opposite them, and call their attention until they make eye contact. Now look at one of the objects, and name it: 'Wow, Ruby, look at the antelope!' Keep looking at it and naming it, occasionally calling your baby's attention and recapturing their eye gaze, until your baby loses interest.

Push both unfamiliar objects close to your baby, and ask them to hand you the antelope. Can they do it? If not, try the experiment from the beginning again, pointing to the antelope this time rather than just looking at it. If your baby still isn't able to pick out the antelope when you ask them for it, try again, this time moving it around as you name it.

Your baby will get better and better at spotting what you're talking about, until they can learn a name through eye-gaze alone with no problem.

Sentences

Following close on the heels of the vocabulary explosion – or
right along with it – comes a new and exciting skill: putting words
together. No other animal can do anything that comes close to what
your baby achieves when they tell you, 'Car gone!', or demands,
'Moh cheese!' Baby starts to make up their own simple, original
sentences from scratch, not just echo familiar word combinations
like 'All gone' or 'Wazzat?' Even if what they say sounds completely
crazy, they are expressing relations between things in a way that
shows amazing brain power. 'Baby cheese' can be a more impressive
utterance than something that sounds relatively sensible like 'Never
mind', if your baby has figured out themselves how to put the words
together to convey their point.

At first your baby will use words stripped of grammatical
endings ('ing', 'ed', and so on), articles like 'a' and 'the' and other
grammatical niceties. This actually demonstrates the size of their
achievement. They are not just parroting familiar sequences of
words, but have broken down the langue they hear into its most
basic parts and are now starting to build their own constructions. If
you have studied a foreign language, you will know that mastering
grammar is every bit as difficult as mastering vocabulary: you need
to get hold not only of conjugations and word endings, but also of
word orders. Your baby does not know what verbs are, or how to set
about trying consciously to conjugate them, but they are constantly
analysing and grappling with grammar whenever you speak to them,
nonetheless.

Your baby will understand the basics of grammar long before they
can use it. Between one and one-and-a-half, they will start to learn
that the order of words in a sentence can affect their meaning, and
that a construction like 'the cat chases the dog' does not mean the
same thing as 'the dog chases the cat'. Soon afterwards, they will
also start to notice and expect appropriate articles, such as 'the,'
to be used in front of nouns ('the dog'), and that there are different
verb endings such as 'ing' ('jumping'), and will be able to understand
sentences more easily when they are present. By the time they are two
they should be well aware of these grammatical bits and pieces. They
will also understand prepositions such as 'with'.

You can check how your baby is getting on with their grammar as soon as they are able to follow simple instructions with some reliability. Try asking them to show you 'crocodile kissing/eating/chasing duck', or something similar. Do they usually show you crocodile eating duck, or duck eating crocodile?

Or you can try saying 'Tassy kiss Mummy' – and then 'Mummy kiss Tassy'. Are they more likely to give you a kiss if you put their name first, and more likely to look expectantly for a kiss if you put your name first?

Quite quickly, your baby will move from their own two-word combinations towards longer strings of words. By the time they are putting three words together, they may not only be able to combine them in an order that makes sense, but also to use their first grammatical trimmings – usually starting with 'ing' on the end of verbs like 'running'. Next come prepositions like 'on' and 'in'. Then 's's at the end of plurals – 'birds'.

A real sign of progress is when your baby, who has been talking about 'feet' for months, switches to 'foots'. They have found a rule, and are determined to apply it: good for them. It's not their fault that English is inconsistent, they'll switch back in time.

Next, baby masters the past tense, saying 'Mummy ran' or 'Mummy runned', or maybe both. Then comes the possessive 's', as in 'baby's hat'. Finally, 'and' and 'the' appear, along with short ways of saying things like 'you'll'.

During this period, your baby is also learning to ask questions. First of all, they will do this just by intonation, by raising their voice at the end of a question – 'Go outside?' – later learning to use interrogative words like 'who', 'what', 'where', 'which', 'does', 'did', etc.

'Why' and 'how' express particularly tricky concepts, and your baby may at first use these words partly as a practice for coming to understand what they mean, or just because they know they get you to talk. Babies whose parents ask them a lot of questions are quicker at learning how to ask questions themselves, so keep your exchanges with your baby interactive!

Keep track of the number of words your baby tends to use in each sentence. Also look at what they are able to express. At first they will be telling you about simple, one-step relations: 'car is red', 'doggy is running', 'Jo fell over'. Later, but not much later, they will be able to express more complex, two-part relations: 'Daddy says the car is red', 'I think the doggy is running', 'I saw Jo fall over'. Your baby is now combining two sentences into one. They will start using 'and' and 'but', and then 'because' and 'if'. By this stage, it's clear that your baby is hardly a baby any more. Though many of their constructions may still sound 'babyish', by age three most children have mastered enough grammatical rules to express all their ideas.

Always **bear in mind the big gap between what your baby can say and what they can comprehend.** For the most part, your job as a brain trainer should be focused not on teaching them to speak but on helping them to understand language: talking will follow, provided you **encourage your baby's efforts at communication. Listen and show enthusiasm** when your baby tries to tell you something – and try really hard to figure out what they are trying to say. Always **show them you've understood,** and provide more language modelling. As well doing whatever they might be trying to get you to do, **repeat and expand what it was they were trying to say:** '"Milk in big mug?" Oh, you'd like some milk in the big mug please, would you? Yes, of course you can have some milk in the big mug! I'll get you some milk in the big mug.' There is no need, at this stage, to correct mistakes, but do phrase baby's message correctly when you repeat it.

Don't worry too much about how your baby pronounces words. Clear pronunciation is really the least significant part of their achievement, and depends more on physical than on mental development. Difficulty with some language noises is expected until at least age six. On the other hand, by three years old, a good deal of what your child says should be comprehensible to people other than their closest family. If speech is still very unclear overall by three, a check with the doctor might be in order, as speech therapy can make a big difference to a young child's clarity.

When will the vocabulary explosion happen?

There is huge variation in the age at which this milestone is reached. The very earliest vocabulary spurts happen around 14 or 15 months, while some babies may be twice that age before their language really takes off.

One of the best ways to predict the timing of a baby's vocabulary spurt is to look at how much language is directed at that particular baby. This is one area where science can firmly say that your efforts as a brain trainer will make a big difference. There are still big individual differences and internal timetables which you can only work with, not cancel out completely, but you can be sure that talking to your baby will help their language skills progress.

There are a number of other factors which psychologists have found predict the timing of language development, though it's possible that these all boil down to the amount of language a baby gets to hear. Baby girls are on average slightly more advanced in language learning than boys. This may be because girl's brains naturally mature slightly more quickly than those of boys. It might also be that parents tend to talk rather more to their baby girls, and roughhouse more with their boys, or that the fact that boys are slightly less mature at birth sets them off on a trajectory of more crying and less social exchange from the beginning. However, the difference between boys and girls is small, and is dwarfed by individual differences between babies. While a team of baby boys is likely to be beaten by a team of baby girls in a language competition, your particular baby boy might be several months in advance of many baby girls of your acquaintance.

First-born children also tend to be about a month ahead of younger siblings in reaching the 50-word milestone, and continue to have slightly larger vocabularies for years to come. Again, this is almost certainly a matter of the amount of time that parents have available to chat to their babies: twins are also at a disadvantage. Even though younger siblings have older brothers and sisters to talk to them as well, teaching language to a baby requires more skill than you might think. **Babies need a bit of 'adult conversation' as much as you do!**

Social class also predicts the speed at which a baby's vocabulary will grow, and for familiar reasons. One American study found that babies in families on welfare on average heard only about a quarter as many words in a year as the babies of professionals. Furthermore, while the babies in professional families had six positive exchanges with their parents for every prohibition, babies in welfare families were told not to do something twice as often as they heard positive encouragement. Of course, a parent on welfare with the time and the will to devote to their baby's language development can still excel the average professional as a brain trainer. But otherwise these huge cultural differences are one of the main factors in creating the gulf in life chances that are already so deeply established between rich and poor children by the end of babyhood.

Remember that perfectly normal babies whose parents are excellent brain trainers reach language milestones across a wide spectrum of ages. It is not unusual for one baby to achieve by two years old what another will not manage until three. This is particularly true when it comes to speech. Some children are just keener to talk than others. Don't worry too much about whether your baby is early or late in their language development. Just keep talking to them and encouraging them to communicate. As long as they seem to progress from month to month, and show interest in listening and communicating, even a baby who seems behind is probably doing fine. On the other hand, if your child does not make eye contact when you speak, or when trying to communicate with you, shows no interest in being read to, and makes little effort to communicate for the sake of it – to tell you about what they see, for example, as well as to ask you for more milk – a health check is in order. The problem may be as basic as a persistent ear infection.

Ten tips for talking to a toddler

1   **Let your baby choose the topic.** Brigid is one of those people who answer 'red' if asked what kind of car she drives. Nevertheless, she is going to have to spend a lot of time discussing vehicles this year, because Baby Tass loves them. Research shows that parents can help language developments by sticking to their babies' chosen topics of conversation.

2 **Expand your baby's vocabulary in the direction of their interests.** While at an earlier stage most parents stick to 'basic' level vocabulary, now is the time to expand in some areas. Tass's sister Ide didn't know the difference between a car and a van at age three, even though by then she could name countless species of flower – we followed her lead when naming objects and talking about them. There are few words that are inherently too advanced for a baby to learn: interest and engagement are what count. By age three, Tass will probably know the names of a wider range of vehicles than Brigid does at 33.

3 **Avoid giving too many commands.** Research shows that babies whose parents spend too much energy issuing business-like instructions and prohibitions learn language less quickly.

4 **Ask lots of questions.** Questions model advanced grammatical forms, and encourage your baby to talk, as well as listen.

5 **Make your questions 'leading'.** As your baby's language develops, the best questions to ask are not ones with a single, simple, one-word, right or wrong answer (What was Billy eating?), but ones that, while quite specific, invite your child to explain, judge and narrate what happened. 'I saw Hannah crying. What was going on there?' However, don't expect your child to answer very open-ended questions like 'What did you do at school today?' or 'Tell Grandma about what we did on holiday'.

6 **Concentrate on comprehension, not correction.** When your baby tries to share with you something wonderful that they have noticed about the world, it's dispiriting for them if you concentrate not on the rainbow they have spotted, but on the mistakes in the language they used to point it out. Research suggests that correcting language does not help at this age. But encouraging communication by showing that you understand and delight in your baby's chat certainly will.

7 **Use eye contact.** Of course, a lot of the time your baby will be rushing around and it will be impractical to look into their face as they talk. But make sure that you sometimes get down to their level to talk to them, and if you have a word you want them to learn, a lesson or an explanation you want them to absorb, take the trouble to get down and eye-to-eye. This will capture their attention and help them remember.

8 **Play games.** Games that involve speaking and understanding are a good way to expand language skills, and have the added benefit of

'testing' your child's budding skills so that you know where they are at and appreciate their growing achievements. Early in this period, you can play games where you ask baby to fetch you the panda, or to show you which toy is the fire engine. Later you can ask them to show you some jumping, or show you the bear tickling the kangaroo. Next, introduce the idea of rhyme, and see if they can find objects with rhyming names. Learn nursery rhymes or poems together, and let them then amaze you by being able to fill in the end words of incomplete lines of verse as you recite them to your child.

9 **Anchor the conversation in the here and now,** but be ready to look further. Talking about relations between things in front of them will help your baby expand their vocabulary and grammar, as they will be able to see what you are talking about. As their language advances, however, you can start to link the here and now with what happened earlier and what might happen later. This will expand the conversation and help them learn about the grammar we use to express the past and future.

10 **Set the scene for conversation.** Try to establish slots in your day when you can really focus on talking with your baby. Call them 'talk-about' times. Meal times, car journeys, ten minutes while you freshen up after getting home from work or a slot during the bedtime routine all work well. If possible, these should be one-to-one chats with little interruption and background noise. If you can keep these established times free for chat as your baby grows into a young child – and even an older child and a teenager – you will be doing something great for their developing intelligence.

Your baby's enjoyment of learning language should be obvious: babies are like poets, loving words for their own sakes. As their mastery increases, keep feeding their passion for language. Introduce and explain, one at a time, complicated grammatical forms, interesting long words, and colourful sayings and turns of phrase. Read them poems and books with interesting language.

Learning language is incredibly complicated, as well as incredibly exciting. In our *Further resources* section we suggest other great books which give more details about the process, and suggest more activities that you and your baby can enjoy together. When it comes to language development, there is a huge amount of science to show that a dedicated brain trainer can make a huge difference – and you can both have fun in the process.

YOUR TURN

▶ Keep talking to your baby as much as you can.

▶ Make sure that as well as labelling objects, you talk about the relations between things in baby's environment.

▶ Keep reading to your baby regularly.

▶ Work hard on understanding what your baby is saying to you.

▶ When your baby speaks to you, repeat what they said and expand it into a fuller and more correct sentence, but don't find fault with their grammar.

▶ Ask lots of leading questions.

▶ Give your baby plenty of time and space to answer your questions or ask questions of their own, showing them that you are listening with all ears.

11

Brain training into early childhood: two years and upwards

In this chapter you will learn:
- *some key facts about how young children think and feel*
- *about educational activities that lay the foundation for school work*
- *good brain training habits that last a lifetime.*

Two- and three-year-olds are barely babies any more, and, in these years before school, your hard brain-training work is beginning to pay off. If you have adopted a brain-training lifestyle, you should notice that your baby has a good attention span, is strikingly inventive in play, and that their close bond to you makes them unusually obedient and engaged for their age. They still learn a lot from playing, but they are also getting more and more from their conversations with you. They are becoming a master of their language, and starting to learn about the world from your explanations, as well as from their own never-ending practical and imaginative experiments.

Understanding how young children think

Once your baby can talk as fluently as you can, is able to run about and climb trees, and occasionally out-argue you, it can sometimes be easy to think of them as a mini-adult who just lacks experience. But children are not mini-adults. In some ways they are smarter than adults, but they remain different from adults in important ways, sometimes right up through puberty. You can train, teach, play with and love your child best if you understand some of these differences.

YOUR CHILD STILL NEEDS HELP DEALING WITH THEIR EMOTIONS

For many years to come, your child will appreciate your help in using the reasoning part of their brain to calm the more primitive, emotional parts when they are frightened or upset.

Often we may think that a child is angry, upset or frightened because they do not understand or know something, and sometimes this is the case. Often, though, the problem is rather that their young brain cannot effectively use the reasoning function of the prefrontal cortex to calm itself. Your baby knows that the robe on the chair isn't really a monster, but their powerful imagination and intense emotions cannot be reined in by their reason.

By all means explain calmly that there is nothing to be afraid of, and encourage your child to try to calm themselves through reason, but do not be surprised or impatient if they do not succeed. Your voice, your gaze, and your cuddles are still crucial to helping them settle their brain chemistry in moments of crisis.

Talk about emotions that they or other people experience – either in reality or in stories. Rehearsing inner experience can be a first step towards being able to master impulses, as well as helpful in the development of empathy and moral behaviour.

Insight: fascination with feelings

Many children become quite fascinated by analysing emotional reactions. We have a lasting memory of Ide at three, chasing after a friend, calling 'Hannah, come back, talk to me, I just want to understand why you don't seem happy!' This interest is helpful in dealing with emotions, and should be encouraged.

Research shows that the ability to control impulsive behaviour is a better predictor of academic success than an IQ score. Once your child has a good understanding of what we mean when we talk about the various emotions, you can try to teach them ways of dealing with their impulses. For example, you can teach them to take a few deep breaths when they are feeling angry or panicky, to sing themselves a song or tell themselves a story when they are feeling impatient, and to cheer themselves up with happy thoughts when they are feeling down. To begin with, go through these motions with them. And always be ready to give them a hug when they need one.

CHILDREN CANNOT FOCUS LIKE ADULTS

A leading child psychologist has described children's consciousness as being more like a lantern glow than a torch beam. To a great extent, children learn by paying attention to everything at once, rather than focusing narrowly on the task in hand.

Almost any parent, hurrying to get out of the house, gets frustrated when their toddler stops to investigate the smell of their new shoe laces, or whether they can slide felt tips under the bathroom door, or the feeling of their woollen sleeves once they've been dipped in the washbasin. In contrast, adults 'close down' their attention to information and ideas that are not relevant to the practical goal of the moment. While you read this paragraph, unused parts of your brain are flooded with special chemicals that effectively switch off interfering signals: your toddler may have to ask you for milk several times before you hear them.

Children's brains have much lower levels of these 'shut down' chemicals than the brains of adults. This fact is illustrated by the fact that if children need to be given a general anaesthetic, they need proportionally much more medication.

Children may feel, all the time, a bit like we feel when we're on holiday in a strange city: we have nothing in particular to get done, no particular route or routine to follow, and can make little sense of much of what we see. On the other hand, we feel acutely sensitive to, and enthralled by, all the new sights, smells and sounds around us.

As a parent, Brigid often has to remind herself of this when she barks at Ide for the tenth time to get her socks on! Remember that this difference between adult and child consciousness can't be got over through any amount of effort on your child's part, or discipline on yours. And when your child is working on something, remember that they can be easily distracted by background noise. If you make any attempts at formal lessons before your child starts school, remember that it is perfectly natural for them to have difficulty focusing for long stretches of time. And try to love and, if you can, share their wonder at all the things in the world, even if right now their lack of focus is driving you crazy.

CHILDREN'S MEMORIES WORK DIFFERENTLY

Have you ever noticed that your little one will never answer fluently when you ask them what they got up to while you were at work? Even school-age children find it hard to tell you about their day on demand. This is because children find it much more difficult to recall memories *at will* than adults do. This is hard to realize, as often very young children seem to have incredible memories for detail of what happened in the past. They can recall fantastic details of what happened a long time back, even when they were very young, but only if they are somehow 'reminded'. They are like novelist Marcel Proust, who found himself swept back in time by the taste of a cake. Be ready to provide cues to prompt your child's recollections.

> **Insight: amazing memories**
> When looking through old clothes, three-year-old Ide told me she remembered wearing a particular dress when we went to the dentist – eighteen months earlier. The dress powerfully 'reminded' Ide of the visit. Children do have great involuntary memories, but struggle to recall what happened at will.

IMAGINARY FRIENDS ARE NORMAL – AND HEALTHY

In the past, parents and psychologists have speculated that having imaginary friends might be a sign of loneliness, social ineptitude, or some other psychological problem. In fact, it turns out that children who have imaginary friends are in the majority, and are actually more likely to be extroverts than children who do not. Apart from that difference, they seem neither smarter nor less smart, and neither more nor less generally 'creative' or rational. On the other hand, children who watch a lot of television, or read or have read to them a lot of stories are rather less likely to have imaginary friends. This difference suggests that stories and imaginary friends may play a similar, and an indispensable, role in the development of a child's mind. They probably help them to develop a deeper understanding of the workings of the world – and particularly the people in it – by adding imaginary experiments to the practical ones they already conduct all day long.

UNDERSTANDING PEOPLE IS HARD WORK

In Chapter 9 we saw how, at around eighteen months, your baby begins to understand that other people have different desires and preferences from themselves. The next, harder, step is to understand that other people's *knowledge* about the world is also different from their own. You get an inkling of how hard it is for them to understand this whenever you play hide and seek. They think hiding their head so that they can't see you will mean you can't see them, even if their whole body is sticking out! Notice also how your young child often expects you to know and talk about events you weren't present for.

Test your young child's understanding of other people

Psychologists have long used the following 'false belief' tests to find out how much young children understand about other people's minds:

For the first test you need a couple of soft toys, a couple of hiding places, and an interesting object. You could use Pooh Bear, Tigger, and something that looks like a honey pot. And then you need to 'do the voices'.

Get Pooh Bear to bring in the honey, chatting to himself about it. 'Oh, I'm looking forward to eating this honey later, after I've seen Piglet about something very important. I think I'd better hide it somewhere so that no heffalumps eat it up while I'm away.' Get Pooh to hide the honey somewhere, and then walk off.

Now Tigger comes in and moves the honey to another hiding place. Make sure your child sees what he's done.

Now bring Pooh back. 'I'm feeling rather peckish. Time for a little something'.

Now, in your own voice – maybe in a whisper – ask your child where do they think Pooh will look for the honey?

Young children will tell you that Pooh will look in the hiding place that really does contain the honey, the place that they saw Tigger move it to. They cannot understand that they only know that the honey is there because they saw Tigger put it there and that, as Pooh did not see Tigger's action, Pooh will expect it to be where he himself hid it.

(Contd)

Children vary quite a lot in the age at which they can predict where Pooh would look for the honey. Most get it right by the age of four. Interestingly, children with autism may not be able to solve the problem until much later, which suggests that quite specific and specialized mental skills are needed to reason about other people's minds and be able to predict their behaviour.

In another experiment, children are shown pencils inside a sweets box. Young three-year-olds are surprised that the box doesn't contain sweets but, if asked, they say that another child will expect there to be pencils, rather than sweets, inside. Even more weirdly, they will deny that they themselves ever thought that there would be sweets in the box. So there seems to be a link between understanding how other people's minds work, and understanding our own minds.

Though first-born children tend to have an edge over second children on most measures of intelligence at this age, second children can make the right predictions about other people's beliefs, and accurately recall their own past beliefs, earlier than first-borns. They obviously profit from all the extra practice negotiating with siblings who have conflicting views and attitudes.

Insight: educational experiments

Ide passed false belief tests early. This might have been because we were always testing her. Toddlers who take such tests and then have their mistakes explained to them afterwards learn from the experience, and are much better able to reason about beliefs in the future.

Talking to your young child

During this period, talking to your child is as important as ever. But by now, instead of focusing on the language in which simple facts are conveyed, your emphasis can shift to explaining and discussing ideas, viewpoints, possibilities and chains of cause and effect. The time for simplification has mostly gone by now. You will notice that, once they have got the hang of basic sentence structures, your child seems to enjoy using tags and bits of language that are not essential to make their point. We tend to expect children to take a very workmanlike attitude to language, using words as efficiently as possible to get across their point, but in fact they show quite a poetic enjoyment of the sound of words for their own sake, and obviously enjoy their mastery of language. Before you know it, instead of just saying 'Give me drink now', your baby might say, 'Speaking of which, I am rather thirsty. I wonder, could I have a drink, do you think?' Look out for the 'unnecessary' tags your child begins to use: 'funnily enough', 'on the other hand', 'imagine that'.

Exercise

Though you might think that exercise is good for body, rather than mind, it is in fact one of the things that we can be most confident will benefit your child's growing brain. Exercise promotes blood flow to the brain, and triggers the production of a synergy of beneficial neurotransmitters. Your child will be noticeably calmer and happier after a good run around. They will also be much readier to learn. Exercise outdoors is likely to bring other special benefits. Try to give your child the chance to play outdoors most days.

Limit television time

There is a growing consensus that any amount of television is too much for children under two. Watching television is too passive. Babies do not learn from it as they do from active engagement with real people and the physical world around them. Research shows that even a specially designed 'educational' DVD seemed to make the babies who watched it less, rather than more, smart.

Television has more to offer as your child grows older, but it also becomes a more insidious danger. Television can teach bad behaviour and may raise stress levels and damage attention span. It can also just waste time that could be used for more intellectually and emotionally stimulating activities. Watching television seems addictive, and the decisions over when to watch can trigger tensions between children and parents. But television is a big part of modern life, so parents need a coping strategy.

TOP TEN TELEVISION TIPS

1 **Make watching television an exception, rather than a habit.** You will avoid regular arguments if your child assumes that television is not usually one of the possible options for how to spend the afternoon. Reserve using it for when your child is ill, when there is a family crisis, and for one-off treats and times when you are desperate for an easy way to keep your child entertained.

2 **When you can, watch with your child.** Watching television can be a valuable experience if you can watch with your child, freezing the action to discuss what's going on and to answer their questions. The programme can be a reference point and source of conversation afterwards.

3 **Look for programmes with a slow pace.** The rapid shot-changes typical of modern shows scramble child's brains and raise stress levels. Look for programmes with long-lasting shots and a calm atmosphere. Classic children's shows from the seventies, such as *Bagpuss* and *Fingerbobs*, are a good choice on this front.

4 **Use DVDs or recorded programmes rather than live television.** This will encourage both you and your child to be selective about what you watch, and to use television at the appropriate moments, rather than switching on at a particular time as a habit. It will also allow you to avoid adverts and inappropriate trailers. The magazine programmes that fill up the gaps between shows on children's television are particularly vacuous and unstimulating.

5 **Encourage re-watching.** All television moves at a pace hard for children to keep up with. Re-watching helps them make sense of and properly digest what they watch.

6 **Look for shows that have lots of language.** Children find television graphics mesmerizing, but there is little to be learned from them. Choose programmes with lots of clear dialogue or a good voiceover.

7 **Suit the show to the moment.** Exposing your child to an action-packed television programme before bedtime is a recipe for sleep problems.

8 **Avoid violence.** Research suggests that even cartoons made for children really can encourage violent behaviour.

9 **Factual programmes can be good.** The striking visuals of a nature documentary, for example, provide a good foundation for conversation and learning about the natural world.

10 **And fantasy can be just as good.** A great film can enrich your child's imaginative life fantastically. Think of the sorts of films that really shaped your imagination as a child. If a show is neither educational nor likely to excite your child's imagination, skip it.

Other new media

We don't yet have any solid research on the benefits and dangers for children of computer games and the internet. To avoid the most obvious danger, **make sure these activities don't replace things we know to be key for the development of intelligence, such as reading, regular exercise, and face-to-face social interaction.**

Beyond that, bearing in mind how little we know, these activities should probably be indulged in moderation. Knowing how to use a computer, software packages and the internet are key skills in the modern world, and you should certainly make sure your child masters them. But always choose educational games and encourage creative and informative web-browsing. The internet is a fantastic resource for a curious child, but make sure that you stay in control of your child's use of it.

Insight: changing cuddle needs

Ide did not look for cuddles much as a young baby. Her need for closeness was probably met by her frequent nursing. But since her weaning, the bedtime cuddle has become her favourite part of the day, and is essential for calming her mind after a hard day's work. It helps calm Brigid, too.

Reading together

Reading to your child has many well-known benefits. It introduces your child to the wonderful world of books, models the reading process, and makes it much more likely that they will soon be a voracious reader themselves. It is usually a calming activity and it strengthens the bond between you and your child. Above all, it is an imaginative experience – and imagination is, as we are discovering, right at the heart of your child's mental life during these early years. Lots of research supports the long-term benefits of reading to your child. Read together for at least 20 minutes on most days if you can, and much longer if you like!

CHOOSING BOOKS

Your child's response is, of course, one excellent guide to the sort of books you should be reading them. But many children enjoy being read to so much that they might just sit still all the way through a lively reading of *What Car* magazine, so you need to exercise some judgement about the most valuable reading experiences. Here are some hints:

1 **Indulge your child's love of repetition, but also try new stories.** Your child enjoys hearing familiar stories – they reassure your child, build their confidence in their ability to make successful predictions, and allow them to practise their amazing memory skills. Your child will build these familiar stories right into themselves, as repetition builds high-speed neural pathways in their brain. Sooner or later you will realize that they know favourite stories word for word from beginning to end. This feeling of mastery and familiarity is good for them, but so are new experiences and stories. Get into the habit of regularly alternating new stories with old, and your child will 'get used' to novelty.

2 **Use your child's interests as a springboard.** This can be particularly important if your child is rather resistant to new stories. Find an angle that draws on your child's interests when choosing new books. Look for books that touch on your child's obsessions (in pirates, fairies or whatever) but also take them beyond them.

3 **Don't underestimate your child.** It is easy to worry too much about books being 'too difficult'. Children enjoy challenges and are much quicker to comprehend advanced and unfamiliar vocabulary and grammatical forms than you might think: after all, they have just learned most of their first language from scratch in a matter of months! You can check that your child is following the story by asking them later whether they can remember what happened at some important point. They will probably surprise you at the level of story they both enjoy and understand. It's good if, on each page, there are a few words your child isn't familiar with. You can tell them the meaning

of some of them, and others they will be able to figure out for themselves.

4 **Aim for lots of questions.** The questions suggested by the story are as important as the story itself. The more your child interrupts you to discuss the story, the better. They will learn a lot, in a particularly joined-up and memorable way, from your answers. Story time should be interactive, not just a matter of listening quietly. Usually, if you get no questions at all, it's because the book is too easy or perhaps just too familiar. Sometimes though, your child is quiet just because they are so wrapped up in the story, and of course that's great too! If your child tends not to ask questions, try asking them some yourself, or interrupt the story to relate it to other stories or to some of your own experiences.

5 **Try non-fiction.** Children love stories, and they should be the mainstay of story time. But non-fiction books for children can also fire the imagination. Not only can they provide a lot to talk about, they can start building general knowledge, and get your child used to the idea that finding out about the world is fun! Look out, for example, for picture or lift-the-flap books about castles, garden wildlife, or costume through the ages.

6 **Look for interesting language.** Choose books which use words that you don't use everyday around the house. Also, don't worry about old-fashioned language. Your child is a language wizard, and will simply add these unfamiliar words and constructions to their repertoire. It's good for them to feel comfortable with unfamiliar linguistic registers.

7 **Look at the pictures as well as the text**. Even once you are reading longer books together, choose ones with interesting illustrations. Bold, simple, stylized pictures are fashionable with publishers of children's books, but these may not be favourites with your children. Illustrations with lots of details are particularly valuable – your child will be able to 'read' the pictures to themselves before they can read the text.

8 **Choose books you will enjoy reading yourself.** Don't be a martyr – you will be more likely to read well and often to your child if you don't find their story-books crushingly dull. It's essential that you both enjoy the story, and there is a huge choice of good books out there.

When should you start teaching your baby to read to themselves?

Babies in their first year can be taught to recognize words. If you and your baby both enjoy language flashcards, and you can make the game a warm and loving activity, that's fine. On the other hand, it is not clear that early word-reading will expand a young baby's world in the way that being able to understand and speak words will do.

There is a big difference between being able to recognize words, and being able to read. Reading involves more than word-recognition. It also involves concentration; concentration narrowly focused in a way that young baby's brains simply are not designed for. Most one-year-olds can be taught to recognize simple words on flashcards, but very few three- or even four-year-olds can sit down and read a book by themselves. If you teach baby to recognize the word 'dog' at age 12 months, you will need to make sure they keep seeing the word regularly for another two, three or four years before they are likely to really use it for themselves. 'Reading' may become no more than a party trick that is forgotten before they get to the age when it can be of use to them.

By four, though, some children will be able to master phonics quite quickly, within a couple of months, and will then be able to read simple books to themselves, with a brain trainer close at hand. And you can start laying the foundations for this moment much earlier.

PHONICS VERSUS LOOK-AND-SAY

The look-and-say method involves learning whole words, through many repeated exposures. You can teach a baby to recognize whole words in this way using flashcards. The problem is that it potentially involves learning hundreds of thousands of words individually, and gives a child no way of dealing with unfamiliar words.

Phonics, on the other hand, relies on breaking up, or decoding, words. So a child, having learned the sounds of the letters of the alphabet, and then of groups of letters that make single sounds, reads out the letters of each word they come across in their book. The two difficulties with this approach in a language like English are first, that the rules governing what sound a letter makes in combination with other letters in the word are complicated and numerous. Second, many of the commonest words are completely irregular. The letters they are made up of do not make up the sound of the word. For example, 'was', 'one', 'thought', and 'said', are all very irregular words.

Ultimately, whichever way your child starts reading, they will end up using a bit of both methods. Everyone needs to spell out the sounds of new words, but everyone also has to learn words like 'one' as a whole word, by heart. But depending on the method you choose, you will start off in different ways.

Very young babies cannot be taught to break down – or spell out – a word into the sounds it is made of. They can, though, learn to distinguish the letters of the alphabet, and to remember what sound each one makes. If you plan to use the phonics method, put up an alphabet frieze as early as you can. Baby will like the pictures even before you start to teach the letters. If you plan to use phonics, it is best to call the letters of the alphabet not by their names, but by the sounds they make ('A' is a short 'a', as in 'apple', not as in 'aid', etc.). Babies can easily learn the sounds of letters in their second year, and this will lay a firm foundation for teaching phonics a couple of years later.

There is no scientifically established 'right' age to teach reading. Most children younger than four will have problems with the focus needed to use the phonics system, but by four should be able to grasp it very quickly.

Insight: match the method to the child

When Brigid was a baby, Pat tried teaching her to read using look-and-say. Brigid angrily tossed away the flash-cards. Later, she had difficulty with reading, and was eventually diagnosed as dyslexic. Dyslexic children will have particular difficulty with the sight-word method, and will find phonics much easier.

Music

Listening to Mozart will not, as it turns out, make your baby smarter – though it may calm them down and put them in a good mood for learning. On the other hand, some research has suggested that actively teaching young children to play an instrument can have a positive effect on some elements of intelligence. Encourage your child to make their own music from as early as possible. Sing together and practise simple instruments. As your child gets older, consider formal music lessons – research suggests they might be a good investment.

Languages

By the time most of us begin to learn our second language, in secondary school, our brains are already passed their best on this front. During the teenage years, learning a new language becomes harder and harder and we pass the point at which it is possible to learn to speak a foreign language with a perfect accent.

Babies' brains begin to specialize in their native language during their first year, and so the earlier you can get your child learning a second (or third, or fourth!) language, the better. Some research suggests that being bilingual may give children an intellectual edge in other areas as well.

The ideal scenario is for your child to speak one language in one place with one person, and another language with another person in another place. That makes it easier to keep the languages separate. However, your child is a language wizard, and in the long term will sort things out perfectly well, even if you can't provide these conditions. If your child spends the day with a nanny who speaks a different language from your own, encourage them to speak the nanny's language between themselves. While this might slow down your child's progress in the home language at the beginning, they will soon catch up, and the temporary delay is well worth the benefits of knowing another language.

Teaching your baby about the world

If you've followed some of our hints, you will be amazed at the way your baby hangs on your words, even if you are talking about a subject in which you might think they would have no interest. Even after they start school, your child will continue to learn an awful lot of what they know from you. Engaged, one-on-one conversation with an adult lays the basis not only for their general intelligence, but also for their general knowledge. It will continue to be their richest source of learning throughout childhood.

During their second or third year, children begin constantly to ask 'why?' Sometimes they ask the craziest 'whys'. 'Why will I get wet if I spill water on myself?' If you **take your baby's questions seriously and make the effort to answer them,** you will be doing some excellent brain training. But you need to understand that sometimes 'why' really means 'tell me more'. That way you won't get frustrated by apparently nonsensical questions, and will be able to interpret the real message behind all the whys: 'I want to learn everything you can tell me!'

You can always **bend the question towards an explanation or a topic you feel would be useful, important and interesting for your child to hear.** They will be happy as long as you keep talking. In discussing why you get wet if you spill water on yourself, you might discuss the difference between solids and liquids, and how water can turn solid if you freeze it, and then take a trip to the freezer to fetch an ice cube, which you can leave to melt on a saucer. The silliest 'why?' can lead to useful 'lessons', if we want to see them that way – lessons your toddler will enjoy because they are a response to their own questions.

All toddlers ask questions to which their parents actually don't have the answers. In some ways, these can be the most enjoyable questions to field. If you have a computer, **show your toddler how you type a word into Wikipedia or Google.** Google images can be particularly useful to help lodge information in your toddler's mind. They will absorb information particularly well if they can choose which images to click on and take a closer look at. If you don't have a computer, make a 'finding out list', and take it with you on a visit to the library, where you can use a computer or the reference books on the shelves.

You will find that young children are most interested in information that can be tied into their interest in the world around them, and that a huge amount of information can be embedded in that way. When you can, **weave interests and information into activities and projects.** Doing is inextricably linked with knowing when we are young. Read a poem about the season you are in, draw or cut out pictures of things associated with that season together, and then go for a walk to look at the seasonal sights, while you talk about why leaves are green in summer and turn red and fall off in autumn.

Don't assume that there are any subjects too complex for your child to take an interest in. With imagination, you can describe almost anything in terms they will understand. It is particularly important that you tell them as much as you can about subjects that you are interested in, and talk to other adults about. That way they will get something out of conversation that isn't even directed at them, and you can chat about your own particular interests. Sooner than you could imagine, you will find yourself learning from your child, as well as teaching them.

From trainer to friend

Helping your child realize their full intellectual potential as they move from babyhood to childhood comes down to understanding, engagement and love. It comes down, in other words, to building a strong, thoughtful and sympathetic relationship. If you develop this kind of relationship with your baby, it will inevitably grow through conversation and closeness as they grow through childhood. Your child's intelligence can flourish and spread its branches ever wider, deeply and securely rooted in nourishing relationships.

Knowing how much love and work you've put in, and how much more your child has done for herself, you will be infinitely proud of them. You should take pride in yourself as a brain trainer, as you progress towards mastery of the most demanding job on earth.

YOUR TURN

▶ Bear in mind that your young child's brain still works differently to that of an adult.

▶ Keep helping your child manage their impulses and emotions.

▶ Limit television watching.

▶ Introduce your child to the computer but control their use of it carefully.

▶ Read together often.

▶ Introduce the letters of the alphabet and the sounds they make.

▶ Start music lessons as soon as you can.

▶ Seize any opportunities you can to expose your child to other languages.

▶ Chat to your baby and tell them everything you know.

▶ Take pride in your developing skill as a brain trainer.

▶ Congratulate yourself on the day that you realize your child is training your brain better than you are training theirs.

▶ Appreciate and enjoy life's most exciting intellectual relationship.

Further resources

WEBSITES

The web is a fantastic source of support and information for parents – and also a notorious fund of misinformation. Be aware of the credentials behind each particular site, and follow links from one reliable source to another.

There are very few good websites that directly deal with how to train your baby's brain. Most of what you'll find on the web on this topic is just hocus pocus, often aiming to get money out of you.

Here are some of the best websites out there to help with your brain training work. They support the sort of brain-training lifestyle choices that can make a real difference.

www.centreforattachment.com
Sound general parenting advice and further resources.

www.babymassage.net.au/
A good website with research and practical advice on baby massage.

www.nd.edu/~jmckenn1/lab/
Website with the latest research and resources on baby sleep.

http://baby-led.rhgdsrv.co.uk/
Website by leading advocates of baby led weaning, with useful information and links.

www.babyledweaning.com
A hilarious baby-feeding site with forum.

www.letters-and-sounds.com
A good site for educational computer games for young children.

www.mumsnet.com
A huge site with lively forums, and advice that is getting better and more scientifically informed all the time.

www.kellymom.com
The best scientifically backed advice on breastfeeding and related issues. If there is an answer out there this website is most likely has it.

www.thebabywearer.com
Amazing introduction to the world of baby slings – you won't believe the range of carriers out there. This is a huge site with thousands of members and a great forum.

www.askdrsears.com
Huge site established by a medical doctor, accompanying best-selling parenting books. Great for health issues.

www.attachmentparentingdoctor.com
Another reliable site by a well-informed paediatrician.

GENERAL PARENTING BOOKS

If you are more interested in practice than in theory, these are some of our favourite general parenting books:

Danks, F., *Nature's Playground: Activities, Crafts and Games to Encourage Children to get Outdoors* (Frances Lincoln, 2006).

Great practical suggestions for outdoor play.

Edgson, V., *The Food Doctor for Babies and Children* (Collins & Brown, 2003).

Goodwyn, S. and Acredolo, L., *Baby Signs: How to Talk with Your Baby Before Your Baby Can Talk* (Vermilion, 1997).

The book to buy if you want more information on baby signing, by the psychologists who developed the concept.

Jackson, D., *Three in a Bed: The Benefits of Sleeping with Your Baby* (Bloomsbury Publishing, 1999).

More info and advice on co-sleeping.

Newman, J., *The Ultimate Breastfeeding Book of Answers* (Random House, 2006).

Pantley, E., *The No-Cry Sleep Solution: Gentle Ways to Help Your Baby Sleep Through the Night* (McGraw Hill Contemporary, 2002).

Rapley, G., *Baby-Led Weaning: Helping Your Baby to Love Good Food* (Vermilion, 2008).

The definitive guide to how to help your baby feed themselves, by the health visitor who developed the concept.

Sears, W. and M., *The Baby Book: Everything You Need to Know About Your Baby from Birth to Age Two* (Harper Thorsons, 1993).

This encyclopaedic guide tells you all you need to know about health, safety, and the basics of child development.

Sunderland, M., *What Every Parent Needs to Know: The Incredible Effects of Love, Nurture and Play on Your Child's Development* (Dorling Kindersley, 2007).

Sound advice and scientifically-backed information about the emotional side of childcare.

BABY BRAIN DEVELOPMENT BOOKS

If you want to learn more about baby brain development, books are still the best source of information. Here are some of the best:

Bloom, P., *Descartes' Baby: How Child Development Explains What Makes Us Human* (Arrow Books, 2005).

More fascinating facts about babies' mental development.

Golinkoff, R. M. and Hirsh-Pasek, K., *How Babies Talk: The Magic and Mystery of Language in the First Three Years of Life* (Plume, 2000).

This book tells you everything you need to know about language development, is readable, funny, and includes great exercises.

Golinkoff, R. M., and Hirsh-Pasek, Kathy, *Einstein Never Used Flash Cards: How Our Children Really Learn – And Why They Need to Play More and Memorize Less* (Rodale Books, 2003).

Great book with a self-explanatory title and a vital lesson to teach.

Gopnik, A., et al., *How Babies Think: The Science of Childhood* (Phoenix, 2001).

Gopnik, A., *The Philosophical Baby: What Children's Minds Tell Us about Truth, Love & the Meaning of Life* (Picador, 2009).

Gopnik, A., et al., *The Scientist in the Crib: What Early Learning Tells Us about the Mind* (Harper Paperbacks, 2001).

CHILD DEVELOPMENT BOOKS

Three books by leading researchers – and great writers – on child development, with fascinating details about how your baby learns about the world.

Hrdy, S. B., *Mothers and Others: The Evolutionary Origins of Mutual Understanding* (Belknap Press, 2009).

Hrdy, S. B., *Mother Nature: A History of Mothers, Infants and Natural Selection* (Pantheon, 1999).

Hrdy's explanation of the evolutionary perspective is clear and absorbing, and will challenge your preconceptions about babies, parents and families.

Louv, R., *Last Child in the Woods: Saving Our Children from Nature-Deficit Disorder* (Algonquin Books, 2006).

A perspective on the psychological risks of a sedentary, indoor childhood.

Index

Image credits

Front cover: © John Lund/Annabelle Breakey/Blend Images RF/
photolibrary.com

Back cover: © Jakub Semeniuk/iStockphoto.com, © Royalty-Free/
Corbis, © agencyby/iStockphoto.com, © Andy Cook/iStockphoto.
com, © Christopher Ewing/iStockphoto.com, © zebicho – Fotolia.
com, © Geoffrey Holman/iStockphoto.com, © Photodisc/Getty
Images, © James C. Pruitt/iStockphoto.com, © Mohamed Saber –
Fotolia.com